OPPOSING VIEWPOINTS® SERIES

Organ Donation

Other Books of Related Interest:

Opposing Viewpoints Series
Genetic Disorders

At Issue Series
How Far Should Science Extend the Human Lifespan?

Current Controversies Series
The Rights of Animals

"Congress shall make no law . . . abridging the freedom of speech, or of the press."

First Amendment to the U.S. Constitution

The basic foundation of our democracy is the First Amendment guarantee of freedom of expression. The Opposing Viewpoints Series is dedicated to the concept of this basic freedom and the idea that it is more important to practice it than to enshrine it.

OPPOSING VIEWPOINTS® SERIES

| Organ Donation

Laura K. Egendorf, Book Editor

GREENHAVEN PRESS
A part of Gale, Cengage Learning

GALE
CENGAGE Learning™

Detroit • New York • San Francisco • New Haven, Conn • Waterville, Maine • London

Christine Nasso, *Publisher*
Elizabeth Des Chenes, *Managing Editor*

© 2009 Greenhaven Press, a part of Gale, Cengage Learning.

Gale and Greenhaven Press are registered trademarks used herein under license.

For more information, contact:
Greenhaven Press
27500 Drake Rd.
Farmington Hills, MI 48331-3535
Or you can visit our Internet site at gale.cengage.com

For product information and technology assistance, contact us at

Gale Customer Support, 1-800-877-4253
For permission to use material from this text or product, submit all requests online at
www.cengage.com/permissions

Further permissions questions can be emailed to permissionrequest@cengage.com

Articles in Greenhaven Press anthologies are often edited for length to meet page requirements. In addition, original titles of these works are changed to clearly present the main thesis and to explicitly indicate the author's opinion. Every effort is made to ensure that Greenhaven Press accurately reflects the original intent of the authors. Every effort has been made to trace the owners of copyrighted material.

Cover photograph reproduced by image copyright Creations, 2009. Used under license from Shutterstock.com.

LIBRARY OF CONGRESS CATALOGING-IN-PUBLICATION DATA

Organ donation / Laura K. Egendorf, book editor.
    p. cm. -- (Opposing viewpoints)
    Includes bibliographical references and index.
    ISBN 978-0-7377-4220-6 (hardcover)
    ISBN 978-0-7377-4221-3 (pbk.)
    1. Donation of organs, tissues, etc.--Popular works. I. Egendorf, Laura K., 1973-
    RD129.5.O738 2009
    617.9'5--dc22

                                                    2008053998

Printed in the United States of America

Contents

Why Consider Opposing Viewpoints?

> *"The only way in which a human being can make some approach to knowing the whole of a subject is by hearing what can be said about it by persons of every variety of opinion and studying all modes in which it can be looked at by every character of mind. No wise man ever acquired his wisdom in any mode but this."*
>
> John Stuart Mill

In our media-intensive culture it is not difficult to find differing opinions. Thousands of newspapers and magazines and dozens of radio and television talk shows resound with differing points of view. The difficulty lies in deciding which opinion to agree with and which "experts" seem the most credible. The more inundated we become with differing opinions and claims, the more essential it is to hone critical reading and thinking skills to evaluate these ideas. Opposing Viewpoints books address this problem directly by presenting stimulating debates that can be used to enhance and teach these skills. The varied opinions contained in each book examine many different aspects of a single issue. While examining these conveniently edited opposing views, readers can develop critical thinking skills such as the ability to compare and contrast authors' credibility, facts, argumentation styles, use of persuasive techniques, and other stylistic tools. In short, the Opposing Viewpoints Series is an ideal way to attain the higher-level thinking and reading skills so essential in a culture of diverse and contradictory opinions.

In addition to providing a tool for critical thinking, Opposing Viewpoints books challenge readers to question their own strongly held opinions and assumptions. Most people form their opinions on the basis of upbringing, peer pressure, and personal, cultural, or professional bias. By reading carefully balanced opposing views, readers must directly confront new ideas as well as the opinions of those with whom they disagree. This is not to simplistically argue that everyone who reads opposing views will—or should—change his or her opinion. Instead, the series enhances readers' understanding of their own views by encouraging confrontation with opposing ideas. Careful examination of others' views can lead to the readers' understanding of the logical inconsistencies in their own opinions, perspective on why they hold an opinion, and the consideration of the possibility that their opinion requires further evaluation.

Evaluating Other Opinions

To ensure that this type of examination occurs, Opposing Viewpoints books present all types of opinions. Prominent spokespeople on different sides of each issue as well as well-known professionals from many disciplines challenge the reader. An additional goal of the series is to provide a forum for other, less known, or even unpopular viewpoints. The opinion of an ordinary person who has had to make the decision to cut off life support from a terminally ill relative, for example, may be just as valuable and provide just as much insight as a medical ethicist's professional opinion. The editors have two additional purposes in including these less known views. One, the editors encourage readers to respect others' opinions—even when not enhanced by professional credibility. It is only by reading or listening to and objectively evaluating others' ideas that one can determine whether they are worthy of consideration. Two, the inclusion of such viewpoints encourages the important critical thinking skill of objectively evaluating an author's credentials and bias. This evaluation will illuminate an author's reasons for taking a particular stance on an issue and will aid in readers' evaluation of the author's ideas.

It is our hope that these books will give readers a deeper understanding of the issues debated and an appreciation of the complexity of even seemingly simple issues when good and honest people disagree. This awareness is particularly important in a democratic society such as ours in which people enter into public debate to determine the common good. Those with whom one disagrees should not be regarded as enemies but rather as people whose views deserve careful examination and may shed light on one's own.

Thomas Jefferson once said that "difference of opinion leads to inquiry, and inquiry to truth." Jefferson, a broadly educated man, argued that "if a nation expects to be ignorant and free . . . it expects what never was and never will be." As individuals and as a nation, it is imperative that we consider the opinions of others and examine them with skill and discernment. The Opposing Viewpoints Series is intended to help readers achieve this goal.

David L. Bender and Bruno Leone,
Founders

Introduction

> *"Organ transplantation is an effective*
> *therapy for end-stage organ failure and*
> *is widely practised around the world.*
> *According to WHO [World Health Or-*
> *ganization], kidney transplants are car-*
> *ried out in 91 countries."*
>
> *—Yosuke Shimazono,*
> *"The State of the International*
> *Organ Trade," Bulletin of the World*
> *Health Organization, December 2007.*

Organ donation affects hundreds of thousands of people and their families worldwide. At the end of October 2008, more than 100,000 people were waiting for an organ in the United States alone. Unfortunately, the number of donors is nowhere near that figure—in 2007, only 14,403 people (living and dead) donated organs. Under U.S. organ policy, donation is an "opt-in" policy—in other words, a person has to agree that he or she will donate organs after death, often indicated by a sticker on a driver's license. Other countries adhere to "opt-out" policies, in which all residents are assumed to agree to become organ donors unless they state otherwise. Also known as presumed consent, opt-out laws can have a significant, though not consistent, affect on organ donation. This introduction looks at laws and attitudes concerning organ donation in different parts of the world.

The United States is not the only country in North or South America with an opt-in, or expressed consent, donation policy. Canada observes similar laws. Approximately 4,000 people are on Canada's organ waiting list. Brazil briefly had a presumed consent policy in 1997, but it was soon repealed. Colombia and Argentina are both presumed-consent nations.

Presumed consent is fairly common in Western Europe as Spain, Norway, Belgium, Italy, Austria, and France all have such laws, though their interpretations of presumed consent vary. For example in Austria, relatives of the deceased may not refuse consent, while in Italy organs can only be removed if the relatives do not object. Just as the laws differ, so do the respective levels of donation in these countries. Spain is most successful in this regard. According to Sheldon Zink, Rachel Zeehandelaar and Stacey Wertlieb, in an article for the American Medical Association publication *Virtual Mentor*, "With 33.5 out of every 1 million residents having organs that are in a condition that allows them to be transplanted after death, Spain has the world's highest rate of actual donation." By comparison, the rates of donation in France and Austria are 22.2 donors per million and 24.8 donors per million, respectively (in the United States, the rate is 21.2 donors per million). Despite these discrepancies, nations with presumed consent laws have been found to have a 25 to 30 percent higher rate of donation than countries with opt-in policies. One such European nation is the United Kingdom, which does not have an opt-out law, although surveys have shown such laws are supported by a two-to-one margin. The donor ratio in the United Kingdom is 12.9 donors per million residents.

Overall attitudes toward organ donation are much different in Asia than in Europe. Despite the size of its population, only 2,000 transplants occur in India each year. Organ donation is also virtually non-existent in Japan. According to an article in the British newspaper *The Independent*, only 40 organs have been donated since 1997. The practice of Shintoism, the dominant religion in Japan, may explain this low number. Under Shinto tenets, it is a crime to injure a dead body—and removing an organ would qualify. Thus, families are much less likely to consent to organ donation. China lacks an organized organ donation system, as explained by David Matas and

David Kilgour in their report, *Bloody Harvest: Revised Report into Allegations of Organ Harvesting of Falun Gong Practitioners in China.* Consequently, as Matas and Kilgour observe, "In this it is unlike every other country engaged in organ transplant surgery." By contrast, Singapore is a presumed-consent nation. With the exception of Muslims, who must opt into the system, all residents of Singapore age eighteen and older are presumed to agree to be an organ donor unless they state otherwise.

Living in a nation where organ donation rates are low does not mean patients—particularly those with enough money—cannot find organs through other means. According to the World Health Organization (WHO), 10 percent of all organ transplants involve travel to poor countries to buy organs. WHO states that 15,000 kidneys are bought and sold on the organ market each year. The organ trade is particularly a serious problem in Asia, as patients from India and Japan frequently turn to organs from China, where the source of the organs is often executed prisoners. Clifford Coonan and David McNeill, writing for *The Independent*, assert, "Hundreds of well-off Japanese and other nationals are turning to China's burgeoning human organ transplant industry, paying tens of thousands of pounds for livers and kidneys, which in some cases have been harvested from executed prisoners and sold to hospitals." It should be noted that such trade is not necessarily illegal, as the organ trade was permitted in Pakistan until 2007, when the government passed the Transplantation of Human Organs and Tissues Ordinance; selling organs was permissible in China until July 2006.

As the above examples show, organ donation policies are far from consistent worldwide. The policies in the United States are especially controversial, as many people question the fairest way to ensure patients receive life-saving organs. In *Opposing Viewpoints: Organ Donation*, the contributors debate issues surrounding organ donation in the following chapters:

What Factors Impact Organ Donors and Recipients? How Can Organ Donation Be Increased? What Are the Ethical Issues Surrounding Organ Donation? and What Is the Future of Organ Donation? Looking at organ donation policies worldwide may be one way to find the answers to these questions.

OPPOSING
VIEWPOINTS®
SERIES

CHAPTER 1

What Factors Impact Organ Donors and Recipients?

Chapter Preface

Organ transplantation is a relatively new medical procedure; it has been less than sixty years since the first successful transplantation from one human to another first occurred. Yet in that short time, the need to find sufficient numbers of donated organs has led to government efforts to ensure proper organ allocation. The first major law in the United States addressing organ donation was the Uniform Anatomical Gift Act of 1968, which established the right of individuals to sign a document agreeing to donate their organs after death.

The next, and more significant, step occurred in 1984, when Congress passed the National Organ Transplant Act (NOTA). This law led to the formation of the Organ Procurement and Transplantation Network (OPTN), which is operated by the United Network for Organ Sharing (UNOS). The purpose of OPTN and UNOS is to make organ allocation fairer and more effective. Every organ procurement organization in the United States belongs to UNOS. UNOS maintains a central computer network that contains the names of all patients waiting for organ transplants. Information on the number of people waiting for an organ is on the UNOS Web site (www.unos.org).

In his book *Organ Transplantation*, David Petechuk explains that public concern over the potential unfairness of the organ transplantation system prompted the passage of the National Organ Transplant Act. He writes: "[In the early 1980s] there were still few concrete laws focusing on the legal aspects of organ donation and transplantation. Already the public was expressing a concern that transplantation would be made available more readily to the wealthy. Furthermore, some suspected that wealthy foreigners were coming to the United

States and essentially buying transplants." NOTA helped address concerns over that issue by banning the sale of organs for transplant.

The United States is divided into eleven geographical regions for the purpose of organ allocation. For example, Region 1 is comprised of Connecticut, eastern Vermont, Maine, Massachusetts, New Hampshire, and Rhode Island. When an organ becomes available, preference is given to patients within the same region. The only exception is for perfectly matched kidneys and for the most urgent liver transplant cases. If no match is found in the region's transplant hospitals, then next on the list are patients in nearby regions.

UNOS and OPTN are not perfect systems, because not everyone who needs a transplant is able to get one, due to a lack of viable organs. The authors in this chapter consider the factors that affect potential donors and recipients.

"Organ donation becomes a consideration . . . only when all life-saving efforts have been exhausted."

Organ Donation: An Overview

U.S. Department of Health and Human Services

In the following viewpoint, the U.S. Department of Health and Human Services (HHS) addresses some of the misconceptions of organ donation. As explained by HHS, doctors will do everything they can to save a potential organ donor's life. The authors also detail the rights of family members of organ donors and address misconceptions about organ allocation. The U.S. Department of Health and Human Services administers more than three hundred government programs and oversees a number of related agencies.

As you read, consider the following questions:

1. As explained by the authors, what is an OPO?
2. What is a donor registry, as defined by the authors?
3. According to the authors, how many organ transplants are performed each day?

U.S. Department of Health and Human Services, "Decision: Donation," 2004, pp. 25–28.

*H*ow *are organs and tissues for transplantation obtained?*

Many organs and all tissues are donated by deceased do-nors—most often a person who has been declared brain dead. A kidney, parts of some other organs, and bone marrow can be transplanted from living individuals—relatives or friends of the recipient or people who choose to be anonymous donors.

Is brain death the same as being in a coma? I have heard that people can recover from a coma. Can people recover from brain death?

A coma and brain death are completely different. A person in a coma still has brain activity and is alive. The person may recover from a coma and possibly regain normal brain func-tion. People who are brain dead have no brain activity. They are dead. Their brain can never recover, but the rest of their body may be kept functioning for a short time by a mechani-cal support system.

Is there an age limitation on whose organs can be trans-planted?

There are no age limitations on who can donate. Both newborns and senior citizens have been donors. Physical con-dition, not a person's age, determines suitability to be a donor. Because of disease or other problems, some people wishing to donate may be ruled medically unsuitable. This determination is best made by transplant specialists at the time someone wishing to be a donor has died.

If I am in an accident, and the doctors know I wish to be a donor, will they still do everything possible to try to save my life?

Yes. Doctors always try everything possible to save a life. In fact, the medical personnel treating an accident victim are not the same as the medical personnel involved in organ do-nation and transplantation. Organ donation becomes a con-sideration—and the local organ procurement organization (OPO) is contacted—only when *all life-saving efforts* have been exhausted.

What is an OPO?

An OPO is a federally designated nonprofit organization responsible for coordinating organ donation and transplantation in a specific geographic area. There are currently fifty-nine OPOs serving the United States and Puerto Rico. In addition to identifying potential donors and obtaining consent where necessary, the OPOs are responsible for the evaluation, preservation, allocation, recovery, and transport of donated organs.

How to Express Interest in Donation

Can anyone declare intent to become an organ or tissue donor?

Anyone can express a wish to become a donor by joining a donor registry, signing a donor card, or indicating intent to donate on a driver's license application. A family may decide to donate the organs of a deceased loved one who has not indicated a choice about donation or who is under age—a child, for example.

A minor usually has to take additional steps to declare his or her decision to be a donor. While requirements vary from state to state, most states require the written consent of the minor's parent or guardian. Many states will only honor the decision of minors over a certain age (for example, minors over the age of 16). Most states consider an 18-year-old to be an adult with respect to the decision to donate; however, this also varies by state. Your local OPO is the best source of information on the requirements in your state.

How do I indicate my wish to be a donor?

You may designate yourself as a donor when you apply for or renew a driver's license or by signing a donor card or joining a donor registry where available. Your local OPO can tell you how to document your donation intentions in your area or state.

What is a donor registry and how do I know whether there is one where I live?

A donor registry is a computerized database of people who wish to be donors when they die. The importance of a registry is that donation intentions can be quickly retrieved 24 hours a day/7 days a week, whereas a donor card or driver's license may not always be available when someone dies. A registry, therefore, provides a reliable way of conveying donation wishes. Donor registries are available in over twenty states. Most, although not all, state registries are operated by divisions of motor vehicles. Ways of joining a registry might include the following: donor card, driver's license, on-line or telephone access, or at public events such as health fairs. Donor registries also provide easy access for people who want to remove their donor designation or place restrictions on the type of organs or tissues they wish to donate. Your local OPO can tell you whether your state or area has a donor registry and how you can join.

The Role of Families

Are families of individuals who have just died but who had not declared an intention to be a donor given the option of donating their loved one's organs and tissues?

Yes. Federal law requires hospitals to report all deaths and imminent deaths to the local OPO. Each OPO works with hospitals in its area to coordinate identification, evaluation, removal, and transport of donated organs. This notification from the hospital allows OPO personnel to determine whether a person who has died is medically suitable to be a donor and to approach family members of potential donors to offer them the option of donating their loved one's organs and tissues.

Can my family be paid for my organs?

No. Organ donation is considered an act of charity by the donor and/or the donor's family, and buying or selling human organs is against federal law.

If I have already decided to be a donor, will my family still get to decide whether my organs will be donated?

In many states, families are asked to provide consent for donation even if the deceased person had indicated an intention to be a donor. Although the decision of a deceased person to designate him or herself as a donor—through a donor card, driver's license, or donor registry—is sufficient consent in all states to allow the donor's organs and tissues to be donated without asking for the family's consent, OPOs in most states ask the donor's family to consent to the donation before proceeding. However, an increasing number of states are passing laws that provide that OPOs must honor the decision of a deceased person to designate him or herself as a donor.

This concept is often popularly referred to as "first person consent" and is based on the belief that the donor's wishes should be paramount and not be overridden by his or her family after the person's death. If the deceased person had not designated him or herself as a donor, the family is asked to make the decision whether to donate. (Generally, even if a deceased minor had indicated an intention to be a donor, the family is asked to consent to the donation.) In first person consent situations, OPO coordinators take great care to talk to the family before the removal of organs to make sure that the family understands and appreciates the donor's desire to save the lives of other people through organ donation.

Does organ donation preclude an open-casket funeral?

No. People who donate organs and tissues can have an open-casket funeral. The surgeons who remove the organs and tissues handle the body in a sensitive way, as they would in any surgery.

Do any religions oppose organ or tissue donation?

Most major religions or religious organizations either actively support organ and tissue donation or leave the decision up to the individual. Those in doubt about their religion's views should talk with their faith leaders.

Good Information Overcomes Myths

According to a 2001 study by the Agency for Healthcare Research and Quality (AHRQ), organ donations increase when families have good information about the donation process.

The study found that:

- Families who knew about a patient's wishes were seven times more likely to donate organs than families who were unsure; and

- Families who met with organ donation professionals about the donation process were more than three times likely to donate organs than families who did not.

U.S. Surgeon General Richard H. Carmona,
remarks to the Joint Commission on Accreditation
of Healthcare Organizations, March 10, 2004.

Facts About Organ Allocation

If I need an organ in order to live, will I be able to get one?

Maybe. Many people who need transplants cannot obtain them because of a shortage of donated organs. There are many more people on the waiting list than there are available organs. As of early 2004, there were nearly 84,000 people on the national waiting list. Every day, an average of eighteen people on the list die waiting for a compatible organ, while an average of sixty-eight receive a life-saving organ transplant.

If my organs are donated, who decides who receives them?

A nonprofit organization under a contract with the U.S. Department of Health and Human Services operates a computerized national waiting list of people who need a life-saving organ transplant. This system matches each wait-listed patient against a donated organ to see which patient is the best match based on factors such as body size, weight, and blood type of the donor and recipient, how sick the patient is, how long the patient has been waiting for a transplant, and where they live in relation to the donor.

Can celebrities or rich or well-connected people jump over others on the waiting list or pay people for their organs?

No. In the United States, the allocation of organs to recipients on the waiting list is based solely on medical and scientific criteria, and on waiting time. The principles of organ allocation are based on equity, urgency, and efficacy—the wealth, age, race, or gender of a person on the waiting list has no effect on when a person will receive a donated organ. In addition, the National Organ Transplant Act of 1984 makes it illegal to buy or sell human organs in the United States.

Costs and Health Issues

If I become a donor, will all my organs and tissues be donated?

You may specify the organs and tissues you wish to donate. Your wishes will be followed. However, if any of your organs are diseased or injured, those organs will not be donated.

I have a history of illness. Are my organs and tissues likely to be of any use to anyone?

At the time of death, OPO personnel will review your medical history and decide whether your organs are suitable for donation. Advances in transplantation and medicines have allowed more people than ever to become donors.

Why is there a disproportionately large number of minority patients on the waiting list?

Minorities are disproportionately represented on the waiting list because certain minority groups are more likely to suffer from diseases that may result in organ failure and require a life-saving organ transplant.

Is there a cost associated with being a donor?

There is no cost to the donor's family or a deceased donor's estate. All costs of removal and preservation of the donated organs are borne by OPOs and are usually passed on to the transplant center and the recipient's insurance company. However, medical costs incurred while attempting to save the life of a potential donor are the responsibility of the donor's insurance company or the donor's family. Costs incurred after a person is determined to be a donor become the responsibility of the OPO.

If I don't have adequate health insurance, can I still be placed on the waiting list?

Given the scarcity of donor organs, transplant surgeons are concerned about transplanting patients who do not have the financial resources to pay for the transplant procedure and follow-up care needed to maintain the organ. In some cases, you might not be placed on the waiting list. However, transplant centers have social workers and financial counselors who work with people being evaluated for a transplant to help them find the necessary financial resources.

Why do I need to tell my family of my decision if I have already recorded my wish to become a donor?

In the event of your death, documentation of your wish to become a donor will increase the chance that you will be a donor. If your family is asked for consent, telling them about your decision to be a donor is the best way to ensure that your wishes are carried out. The death of a loved one is a very difficult time for a family, and knowing the wishes of the deceased makes it easier for them to decide about or accept donation.

| "Organs should be allocated in ways that achieve their best, most efficient usage."

Organs Are Not Allocated Properly

President's Council on Bioethics

In the following viewpoint, the President's Council on Bioethics contends that changes need to be made to the organ allocation system in the United States. The council asserts that the current policy relies too heavily on geography and on how long a recipient has been waiting for an organ. According to the council, the allocation system should be revamped to give greater weight to factors such as the ages of the recipient and donor, and to the long-term benefits of the potential recipients. The President's Council on Bioethics advises the administration on bioethical issues and explores advances in biomedical science and technology.

As you read, consider the following questions:

1. In the view of the council, how did the passage of the National Organ Transplantation Act signal a new phase in organ allocation?
2. According to the council, what is the most heavily weighed factor in kidney allocation?

President's Council on Bioethics, "Organ Transplantation: Potential Policy Recommendations," 2006.

3. Why would giving preference to young patients not be discrimination against older patients, as explained by the council?

This [viewpoint] explores a series of focused policy recommendations that work within the general ethical framework of the current [organ donation] system. These recommendations envision reforms that serve one or more of the moral goals of the current system, without violating any of the principles integral to its overarching moral framework. These recommendations are offered as potential recommendations; they are intended to spur and direct Council discussion and to assess where the Council might pledge its support. For those recommendations that do seem to have broad support, the staff will develop them further and in greater detail. . . .

[One] category includes two policies that would better serve the aims of equity and utility in organ allocation: first, by taking measures to mitigate geographical inequities in organ allocation, and second, by reforming the criteria that govern kidney allocation. . . .

Improving Organ Allocation

Utility and equity are the central moral ideals that govern the existing system of allocating organs to those on the public waiting list. The practical application of these moral ideals is a complicated, ongoing process, rooted in both certain historical realities about how organ transplantation took shape in the United States and in certain clinical realities about the viability and compatibility of human organs.

Both procuring and allocating organs originated as local practices, shaped by and directed to the needs of local and later regional communities. In 1984, the passage of the National Organ Transplantation Act by Congress signaled a new phase in the evolution of allocation policy: organ transplantation was embraced as a medical innovation of national—

rather than local or regional—significance, as was the need for a more ordered, principled approach to securing and distributing the precious resource of human organs. Subsequent legislative and regulatory initiatives, by Congress and the Department of Health and Human Services, have served to articulate and to buttress three ethically relevant norms: first, in organ allocation, the operative sense of community should be the national (rather than local or regional) community; second, organs should be allocated in ways that achieve their best, most efficient usage; and third, beyond effective usage, the most important criterion in allocating human organs should be patient need.

In recent years, there has been laudable progress in the effort to bring the system of allocation into conformity with these norms. For example, reforms in the allocation algorithms for livers and lungs have tilted the balance of criteria toward urgency of patient need and, as a result, there are now fewer deaths on the waiting list for these organs and geographic disparities have been lessened. Nonetheless, so-called "accidents of geography" remain; where a person is registered as a transplant candidate continues to be a potent factor in determining whether one ultimately receives an organ or not. To the extent that organ viability is critical to the efficient, effective use of these scarce resources, geography will remain a constraining factor in the allocation of human organs, especially hearts. Yet the geographical inequities that persist in current practice are not dictated entirely by the demands of utility. In some cases, the most worthy recipient, judged by criteria of physiology, age, medical urgency, or waiting time, is not getting an available and viable organ, or is waiting much longer for such an organ, simply because they live in the wrong place.

Clearly, there are significant challenges and obstacles that mark the path toward greater geographical equity in the system. Moreover, the original and now traditional practice of

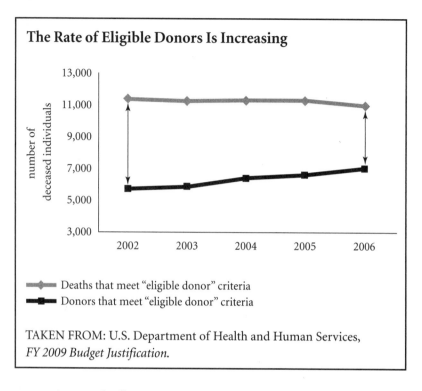

The Rate of Eligible Donors Is Increasing

- Deaths that meet "eligible donor" criteria
- Donors that meet "eligible donor" criteria

TAKEN FROM: U.S. Department of Health and Human Services, *FY 2009 Budget Justification.*

procuring and allocating organs within the same local community is deeply entrenched, in part, because it has served legitimate community needs—and served them well. For sound ethical reasons, however, the nation has embraced geographical equity as the most defensible basis for allocating human organs. In deference to this ideal, the Council could urge UNOS [United Network for Organ Sharing] and the Department of Health and Human Services to continue to explore and institute reforms that would ensure that allocation serves the needs of patients, unfettered by accidents of geography.

Factors in Kidney Allocation

At present, the factor weighed most heavily in kidney allocation, beyond physiological compatibility between donors and recipients, is waiting time. While this criterion serves equity in an obvious sense, giving waiting time such a high importance in allocation risks undermining utility and equity in other crucial ways. To begin with, it means that the value of receiving an organ is diminished by waiting for years on dialysis in order to receive it; the result is that we are getting fewer quality years out of the organs we transplant. We are also transplanting organs to a comparatively older rather than younger set of patients with renal failure. The Council could recommend reforming the kidney allocation system to give greater relative weight to other factors. Such factors might include:

Age of Recipient: Already, we give priority in kidney allocation to pediatric patients. The Council could recommend expanding this principle to benefit comparatively young, nonpediatric patients—for example, by assigning points for age in a sliding scale, such that as age increases, the points in the algorithm assigned for age decrease.

Age Relationship of Donor and Recipient: Under the current allocation system, organs from 20-year-old deceased donors are sometimes transplanted into 60-year-old recipients. The Council could recommend developing a policy requiring that donors and recipients be of a certain proximate age: for example, a 50-year-old on the waiting list could be eligible for organs only from donors within a decade of his or her age (i.e., 40- to 60-year-olds).

Long-Term Benefit: The Council could recommend giving greater relative weight to donees who stand to benefit the longest from receiving a kidney transplant.

Net Benefit: The Council could recommend giving greater relative weight to donees who would likely receive the greatest net benefit from a kidney transplant compared to continuing with dialysis. Such a net benefit calculation could also take into account the comparative quality of life on dialysis versus life after transplantation.

The Current System Is Not the Best Approach

Each of these proposed reforms of course invites its own criticisms and problems—including the problem of shifting from the current system to a reformed system. Any system of allocating a scarce resource stands to benefit some and thus disadvantage others. But there are sound reasons to conclude that the current system is not the only way, or the best way, to serve the goals of utility or equity in kidney allocation, and that it will serve these goals even less well as the size of the waiting list continues to grow. In particular, by giving some relative preference to the young, a reformed allocation system would attempt to ameliorate some of the inequities of nature (such as getting end-stage renal disease in one's twenties) in addition to maximizing the benefits received from transplanted organs; it would not discriminate against the old, but recognize that in allocating a scarce resource, we need to do so based on some moral understanding of whose claims are the weightiest.

"Even when we control for causes of death, facts about social structure and demography will still affect the [organ] procurement rate."

Demographics Can Impact Organ Donation

Kieran Healy

In the following viewpoint, Kieran Healy asserts that demographic factors can significantly impact the rate of organ procurement. These factors include race, poverty, and education levels. In addition, Healy argues, the methods used by organ procurement organizations (OPOs) can also influence the willingness of people to donate organs. Healy is a professor of sociology at the University of Arizona.

As you read, consider the following questions:

1. According to the author, what percentage of people waiting for kidney transplants are African American?
2. As explained by Healy, why do hospitals play an important role in the organ procurement process?

Kieran Healy, *Last Best Gifts: Altruism and the Market for Human Blood and Organs.* Chicago: The University of Chicago Press, 2006. Copyright © 2006 by The University of Chicago. All rights reserved. Reproduced by permission.

3. By how much does the procurement rate increase when OPO spending increases by 10 percent, according to Healy?

As with research on motivated altruism in general, researchers have discovered (and rediscovered) the importance of situational factors to organ donation without systematically pursuing them. An important early study by Roberta Simmons found that living kidney donors were more likely to have been asked in person to give than were nondonors. A more recent study found that female relatives were more likely to donate a kidney than were male relatives, possibly because women were more likely than men to be asked to donate. In the case of cadaveric donors, the importance of the person-to-person request process has been subject to increasing attention from researchers.

A Look at Several Demographic Factors

We can think of variation in rates of organ procurement, then, as being shaped by two kinds of forces: features of OPOs' [organ procurement organizations'] catchment areas and characteristics of the OPOs themselves. The research literature on organ donation and donor motivation suggests that even when we control for causes of death, facts about social structure and demography will still affect the [organ] procurement rate. In particular, population density, racial composition, the poverty rate, and the average degree of educational attainment in an OPO region might all be important.

Population Density. Some OPOs administer relatively small, densely populated regions. Others service huge areas. While the New York Organ Donor Network procures donors from the millions of people concentrated in the five boroughs of New York City, the territory of the LifeCenter Northwest Donor Network includes nearly all of Washington, Idaho, Montana, and Alaska. Potential donors must be located quickly and transported to a suitable hospital. This is easier to accomplish in a densely populated area. If OPOs are responsible for large, sparsely populated regions, their procurement efforts may well be focused on any more densely populated areas within it. Even so, the number of donors procured per thousand evaluable deaths will most likely be lower.

Race. Support for organ donation varies a great deal by race. Blacks are less likely to donate than whites, less likely to sign donor cards or discuss donation with their families, and less likely to support the idea of organ donation generally. At the individual level, African American families refuse consent to procure organs at much higher rates than members of other ethnic groups, and there is evidence that their refusals are rooted in a set of concerns that differ from those of white families. Beliefs that the transplant system is unfair to minorities, a more general distrust of the medical system, or ineffective methods of request on the part of OPOs have all been suggested as possible explanations. The general position of African Americans in the transplant system is also relevant. Recent studies have found that blacks face several structural barriers to organ transplantation. Incidence of hypertension and end-stage renal disease is highest in the black population, and African Americans comprise 34 percent of those on dialysis and 30 percent of those waiting for kidney transplants. Yet blacks are much less likely than whites to express an interest in, be listed for, or receive a transplant. As it stands, the reluctance to donate among minorities is a fact of OPOs' operating environments. The higher the percentage of African Americans in an OPO's service population, the lower its procurement rate is likely to be.

Poverty Rate. When a potential donor becomes available, procurement must happen quickly. If the donor is an accident victim, she must be found and brought to a hospital quickly and placed on a ventilator. A procurement team must be able to get to the hospital quickly and do the surgery to procure the organs. The better the facility the more efficient the process will be. OPOs that serve wealthier areas are more likely to have the right resources and facilities available to them and the hospitals they work with. We should therefore expect that OPOs serving poorer counties will tend to procure fewer of the potential donors that become available.

Education. Survey data show a higher level of support for organ donation among more educated people. As discussed above, there is a gap between abstract support for organ donation and the actual decision as a next of kin to allow procurement to go ahead. But on the whole, its effect should be positive: we should still expect OPOs serving more educated populations to do better on average than others, because they ought to encounter fewer obstacles when attempting to secure consent from donor families.

Organizational Impacts on Donation

Despite their importance, these structural and demographic forces cannot be the whole story. Of central interest to us is the role played by the OPOs themselves. We can think of three broad features of an organization that will affect its ability to accomplish its goals. These are its resources or overall budget; its scope or reach within its environment; and its policies and practices as it carries out its task.

Organizational Resources. Were there no OPOs, there would be no organ donors. Donor procurement is a resource-intensive procedure requiring rapid and coordinated organizational action. Dedicated facilities for procurement make the process more efficient on a number of measures. The point should generalize. Larger, resource-rich OPOs should be expected to do better on average than smaller ones. We can use OPO administrative spending per annum to capture this idea. When measured relative to the number of potential donors, OPO spending indexes the resources that the organization brings to the procurement process.

Organizational Scope. OPOs are not the only players in the procurement process. Most donor-evaluable deaths occur in hospitals. In some cases, the OPO will have a staff member working at the hospital. More often, a member of the hospital staff has the task of contacting the OPO to let them know that a potential donor has become available. Hospitals thus play a key role in the procurement process. OPOs may make referral agreements with hospitals. The more hospitals an OPO has referral agreements with, the more donors it is likely to procure. This is a measure of an OPO's reach, or scope. Separate from spending, it captures the extent of the OPO's coverage and the range of its ties to potential sites of donor procurement. Because not all hospitals will have the right kind of patients, we count the number of referrers per thousand in-hospital evaluable deaths.

Organizational Policy. Beyond their varied resources and reach, OPOs differ in their procurement policies and consent practices. Although all OPOs are interested in getting people to carry donor cards, donor families are central to the procurement process, as it is they who give or refuse consent for donation. Convincing families to agree to donation is a delicate affair. Successful organ procurement should be related to the strategies adopted by OPOs. This idea is consistent with broader social-science research that seeks to situate altruism within an organizational and institutional framework and with other findings about charitable donation, which have shown that whether and how one is asked to give is a better predictor of giving than the individual characteristics of donors. Within the transplant field, researchers find that families rarely suggest donation of their own accord and that "educational interventions for health care professionals and a coordinated requesting process that includes the organ procurement organization and hospital personnel result in a higher number of donations."

OPOs differ in their policies regarding whether and how families or next of kin are asked for permission to donate. Although in principle (and in law) a signed organ donor card is sufficient to justify procurement, in practice, as we have noted, the situation is more fluid. There is substantial variation in consent policies. Specifically, OPOs vary in how willing they say they are to try to obtain consent. Some, for example, may be more willing than others to suggest that the wishes of the deceased be respected even if the family has reservations about donating. The expectation is that the stronger the policy, the higher the procurement rate. . . .

The Impact of Education and Spending

Increasing the percentage of the population that is college educated has a negative effect on procurement. This is unexpected, as we know that there is substantially stronger support than average for organ donation among more educated people. Nevertheless, it is not clear that this effect would show up here, given that we are measuring effects at the OPO rather than the individual level. We might think that better-educated people are less likely to die in circumstances conducive to procurement—in automobile accidents, for example, or from gunshot or stab wounds. Recall, however, that the outcome measure is the procurement rate among evaluable deaths, rather than all deaths or the live population. Selection into the donor pool is therefore already controlled for and cannot explain the negative effect of education. One possibility is that the effect is the result of outlying observations. Education is more sensitive than the other variables to the presence of a small number of cases in the data, but even when these cases are dropped one by one its effect remains negative. The finding seems robust given the data but remains to be fully explained.

Taken together, the environmental variables explain about a third of the observed variation in the procurement rate.

Some African Americans Distrust Government Organ Allocation

[Some African Americans are] skeptical about government distribution of organs. J.D., a 38-year-old police officer, posited, "You know how the government is, they might be giving African Americans' organs to people with a good deal of money—to the rich. Predominantly White Americans may get most of them. I think White America would benefit from that." L.J., a 27-year-old medical records clerk, was alarmed by the idea, opining, "it's almost like having a dictatorship almost. One should still be able to decide—or one's family should be able to decide what they can do with their body." When asked whether mandatory donation would resolve the organ crisis, her response was, "No. They would give them all to White people."

Michele Goodwin, Black Markets: The Supply and Demand of Body Parts. *New York: Cambridge University Press, 2006.*

When we add in the three organizational measures, we can explain more than half of the variance. These measures show some interesting effects. OPO spending per capita is positively and significantly related to the procurement rate. (As with population density, we use the logarithm of spending here.) A 10 percent increase in spending raises the procurement rate by nearly nine-tenths of a point. The number of referring hospitals per thousand evaluable deaths also has a strong effect on procurement. A 5 percentage point increase in the density of referrers raises the procurement rate by about three-quarters of a point. These results strongly suggest that the organizational resources of OPOs play a very important role in determining the procurement rate.

In contrast, the measure of OPO policy shows no strong effects. The variable measures an OPO's willingness to procure in hypothetical circumstances where consent is ambiguous. The consent policies of OPOs have been assumed to play an important role in the procurement process, so it is surprising to see so little effect here. Two interpretations suggest themselves. It may be that in fact the consent policies of OPOs do not have a strong effect on the procurement rate. The original survey instrument took considerable care to ensure accurate responses, however. A second interpretation is that, although the survey is accurate as far as it goes, it did not pick out real organizational practices. Discussion of hard cases, whether hypothetical or real, is a staple of the bioethics literature, and of course teasing out these cases can teach us about the scope and limits of our ethical ideas. But these kinds of dilemmas may have little to do with the everyday work of organ procurement. What-if questions about the limits of procurement policy might not be a helpful way to understand what is happening inside OPOs.

Changing the Approach to Organ Procurement

Evidence from other sources supports this idea. From the mid-1980s to the mid-1990s, the South Carolina Organ Procurement Agency (SCOPA) consistently ranked in the bottom half of OPOs in terms of procurement rates. This was partly due to its geographical location, a poorer than average area with a higher than average black population. Our findings so far ... make its poor performance unsurprising. Since 1997, however, this OPO has increased its donation rate by 83 percent as a result of a series of changes in the management of the procurement process. Consistent with the ideas developed [here], SCOPA invested more money and people in the procurement process, increasing its field staff from eight to twenty-one employees. But it also changed its procurement methods. The key innovation was to decouple the moment donor families were told about the brain death of the patient from the moment they were asked to consent to donation. Tasks previously assigned to a single procurement coordinator—hospital liason, family support counselor, donor clinician, recovery coordinator, and aftercare coordinator—were assigned to separate employees, each with an appropriate professional background. The OPO's organizational mission had been simply to procure as many high-quality donor organs as possible. During the restructuring, SCOPA changed its name to LifePoint and added a "family support service." The goal of this part of the organization was "to insure that families of dying patients . . . made well-informed decisions about donation and had timely bereavement counseling and follow-up." A crucial aspect of the reorganization was that the person who explained to families that their loved one was brain dead, and who spent a considerable amount of time (perhaps a whole day) helping them with this realization, was no longer the person who requested consent for donation. Within five years of the new methods' introduction, consent rates were about 85 percent, close to the proportion of the population that survey data suggests supports organ donation in the first place.

The implications of these organizational changes are striking. On the narrow question of the measurement of OPO policy, they suggest that asking detailed questions about an OPO's willingness to procure donors under adverse circumstances (e.g., in the face of opposition from the families) might not be very informative. LifePoint's success was due to strategies designed to make it easier for shocked and grieving families to understand and fully support the procurement process. By splitting the information-provider role from the consent-request role, they ensured that the person providing families with information about brain death (and helping them manage for the day in the hospital) would not be perceived as having an ulterior motive. Thus, families are carefully managed by the organization in a way that shepherds them toward the vital moment when consent is requested.

These results show the value of looking at organ donation as an organizational problem. Donation is an exceptional, one-shot event for donor families, but it is a stable and mostly predictable circumstance from an organizational point of view. It depends on exogenous environmental forces, but it is also strongly affected by the resources and scope of the procurement agency. The social production of altruistic action—the provision of a stable supply of voluntarily donated hearts, livers, and other organs—can be thought of as a resource-extraction problem that organizations solve more or less effectively. From this perspective, the individual capacity for altruism and the social organization of procurement are not separate questions but rather two aspects of the same process. As organizations create "contexts for giving" they elicit altruistic action differentially across populations. Rather than simply discovering preexisting populations with dispositions to give, they help create their own donor pool.

"Many people with disabilities are . . . denied evaluation and referral for transplantation at the primary care level."

The Organ Transplant Process Is Biased Against the Disabled

Joint Commission on Accreditation of Healthcare Organizations

In the following viewpoint, the Joint Commission on Accreditation of Healthcare Organizations (JCAHO) argues that disabled people face bias in the organ allocation system. JCAHO asserts that hospitals and transplant professionals wrongly assume that people with physical and mental disabilities are incapable of following complicated post-transplant regimens. According to the commission, the health care community needs to support the disabled and their families. JCAHO is a nonprofit organization that accredits and certifies more than 15,000 health care organizations in the United States.

Joint Commission on Accreditation of Healthcare Organizations, "Health Care at the Crossroads: Strategies for Narrowing the Organ Donation Gap and Protecting Patients," *The Joint Commission*, 2004, pp. 21–23. © 2008 The Joint Commission. All Rights Reserved. Reproduced by permission.

As you read, consider the following questions:

1. As explained by the Joint Commission, why did the second hospital refuse to give Sandra Jensen a heart/lung transplant?

2. According to a survey cited by the authors, what percentage of disabled people and their family members believe that stereotypes are the reason for denying them transplants?

3. What percentage of people who responded to the survey, as stated by the commission, lack full insurance coverage for transplantation care?

The world of organ transplantation is . . . a harsh environment for people with mental and physical disabilities. When this new treatment option was first introduced, individuals with disabilities were automatically excluded from consideration for transplantation. The basis for this exclusion was the perception of worthiness against the reality of scarcity—"a valuable organ for an unvalued life."

The Disabled Face Several Hurdles

Since passage of the Americans with Disabilities Act [ADA] and the establishment of related federal regulations, discrimination against persons with disabilities in medical treatment is prohibited. But, despite the legal protections offered to persons with disabilities, many still face significant hurdles to being assessed for, wait-listed, and eventually receiving donor organs.

The first earnest—and very public—fight for transplantation for persons with mental disabilities began in 1995. Sandra Jensen, a 34-year-old woman with Down syndrome and a terminal cardiac condition, was recommended for a heart/lung transplant by her attending physician as the only means to save her life. Her insurer, MediCal, approved the request with the requirement that it be performed at one of its two

Misconceptions About the Intellectually Disabled

Sixty percent of transplant centers reported that they'd have serious concerns about giving a kidney to someone with mild to moderate intellectual disability apparently based on fears that these patients can't handle the complex post-transplant care. The facts are exactly the opposite: People with intellectual disabilities who have been lucky enough to get a transplant do as well if not better than non-disabled people.

Timothy Shriver, "No Room at the Inn,"
The Washington Post, December 25, 2006.

designated California transplant centers. Both centers refused Sandra. One of the hospitals denied Sandra's request without ever having met or examined her. The position of this hospital was that people with Down syndrome were not appropriate candidates for heart/lung transplants. The other hospital did consider Sandra's case; however, while finding no medical basis for excluding her, it determined that she would be unable to understand the procedures and to follow complex medical regimens.

The inability to follow medical regimens and the lack of support systems are the two criteria commonly used to screen out patients with disabilities from transplant waiting lists. In Sandra's case, they picked on the wrong patient. According to Dr. William Bronston, who worked alongside Sandra to defend her cause, Sandra was highly accomplished, working on behalf of disability rights causes and living independently all of her adult life. She had a close-knit family and a large network of friends and colleagues. In fact, with the help of these friends and colleagues, and her own determination, Sandra's fight became national news. The pressure of the publicity eventually drove one of the hospitals into submission. Sandra received her heart and lung transplant—the first of its kind in the world—and opened a window for the disability community.

There are, of course, patients for whom a denial of transplantation may be justified—perhaps if only temporarily—if they cannot follow the necessary post-transplant regimens and lack necessary support systems. The legacy of Sandra's case is that, in the words of her transplant surgeon, "We should never judge who is worthy by a generalization. Each person deserves to be evaluated as an individual."

Improving Access for Disabled Patients

Since Sandra, others with disabilities have received life-saving or enhancing transplants. The exact number is not known; however, what is known is that many people with disabilities are still denied evaluation and referral for transplantation at the primary care level.

Even if that hurdle is cleared, these individuals may still be excluded from transplantation by transplant professionals who lack specific expertise in evaluating and determining the capabilities of disabled persons to comply with post-surgical regimens.

In 2003, the National Work Group on Disability and Transplantation was formed to address issues of access, equity and training in order to—in part—promote better understanding and treatment for persons with mental and physical disabilities. The Work Group is also pursuing a national research agenda to determine the level of access persons with disabilities have to transplantation in relation to their needs.

An initial Web-based survey of persons with disabilities and/or their family members, which was administered by the Work Group, found that 80 percent of the 205 respondents believe that people with disabilities are denied access in obtaining organ and tissue transplants because of stereotypes and negative attitudes toward the physically and mentally disabled populations. For these respondents, there is both good news and bad news. Of the 139 respondents that were referred to a transplant center for evaluation, 55 percent were told transplantation was an option; while 45 percent were told it was not an option. For the latter group, some of the reasons given were, ". . . because she has Down syndrome." And, ". . . if he were normal like us, he'd be a great candidate . . ." One respondent—after their son was denied a liver transplant despite a determination of medical suitability—enlisted the Justice Department's help and was able to get the denial reversed.

Perceptions of "worthiness" are not simply an issue for the medical community and transplant system gatekeepers; it is an issue for families of disabled persons as well. Among the survey respondents, 44 percent of families did not pursue seeking a referral to a specialist or transplant center from their primary care physician. Perceptions relating to quality of life and the value of that life color the expectations and decisions of many family members and caregivers of disabled persons, and buttress the existing biases in society at-large. Disincentives created by financial barriers loom large as well—58 percent of survey respondents reported having no coverage, or only partial coverage for transplantation care.

With the proper recognition and support of the health care community, people with disabilities, as well as their families and advocates, can improve access to transplantation by becoming organ donors themselves. Increasing organ donation ultimately means there will be more organs available for everyone.

| "It is increasingly important to raise awareness of the need for more black and Asian donors."

Religious Beliefs Can Impact Organ Donation

Elizabeth Lynch

A misunderstanding of religions' views on organ donation has led to a shortage of organ donations from minorities, Elizabeth Lynch argues in the following viewpoint. According to Lynch, none of the major religions prohibit organ donation, although consultation with a spiritual leader might be required first. However, Lynch contends, minority ethnic populations may not be aware of these teachings, and therefore awareness needs to be raised to help alleviate the organ shortage. Lynch is a journalist who has written numerous articles for Nursing Standard *and other medical publications.*

As you read, consider the following questions:

1. How do Orthodox Christians view organ donation, according to Lynch?

2. According to the author, what Hindu niyama can be interpreted as supporting organ donation?

Elizabeth Lynch, "Faith in Transplants," *Nursing Standard*, vol. 19, April 27, 2005, pp. 24–27. Copyright RCN Publishing Company Limited © 2005. Reproduced by permission.

3. As stated by Lynch, what did the UK Muslim Law
   Council decide in 1996?

Every year hundreds of people die in the UK [United King-
dom] while waiting for an organ transplant. But the death
toll would be reduced significantly if religious and cultural
fears of organ donations were overcome.

The need for organ donation is high among minority ethnic groups. According to UK Transplant, a special health authority with a remit for matching and allocating donated organs, people of black and Asian origin are three to four times
more likely to need a kidney transplant than the rest of the
population. This is because those of south Asian and Afro-
Caribbean origin are particularly susceptible to diabetes and
high blood pressure, which often result in kidney and heart
failure.

Reaching Ethnic Donors

For a transplant to be successful it is important that the blood
group of the donor and recipient is matched. With kidney
transplants, tissue type matching is also important. The closer
the match the better and a close match is more likely if the
individuals are from the same ethnic group—tissue types tend
to be incompatible between ethnic groups.

Although the highest number of organ transplants—
2,867—was recorded [in 2004], 443 people died while waiting.
Of those, one in seven was from a minority ethnic group.
Given the need for more organs to be donated, why is there
this shortfall? Sue Sutherland, chief executive of UK Transplant, says; 'The problem is that people in general, whatever
their culture, do not talk about organ donation with their
families. But because of cultural and language barriers, black
and Asian communities are even harder to reach.

'Many think their religion forbids organ donation, but
none of the major religions in the UK objects to organ donation and transplantation.'

Cynthia Davis, Afro-Caribbean organ donation awareness programme manager for Dulwich Hospital in London, has been looking at this area for three years.

Christian Views on Organ Donation

'There is a reluctance by minority ethnic people to offer their organs for donation. From speaking to people from religious groups, I think many have issues over whether this is the right thing to do. They think: "I have been born with these organs, God has given them to me, they are for my use and I don't think it is right to pass them on to anyone else." So there is an issue of ownership.'

Some Christians want to die whole, so there can be issues with the mutilation side of organ donation. For some other faiths, the followers are taught that they will rise again in the next life and will be raised as a whole person. Ms. Davis argues that these views stem from a lack of education and lack of understanding of what organ donation entails. In many religious groups, as well as people who have very strong faiths, there is a belief that if something is wrong with them, God can heal them and they should wait for that healing.

UK Transplant produces a series of booklets setting out different religious views on organ donation and transplantation. Christian ethos, for example, preaches sacrifice and helping others, and so a decision to donate organs is seen as positive.

Christians are encouraged to help others in need. They look on organ donation as an act of love and a way of following the example of Jesus. For members of the Orthodox Christian faith, donations of organs after death is generally allowed as long as respect is shown to the body before, during and after the procedure and as long as the organs are donated for altruistic reasons.

All mainstream Protestant denominations support organ donation and see it either as an individual choice motivated by compassion or encourage it as an act of charity. Most Pentecostal and evangelical churches are also in favour of organ donation.

Hindu and Buddhist Views

There is no religious law that prohibits Hindus from donating their organs or tissues. Life after death is a strong belief of Hindus and is a continuing process of rebirth. This could be seen as reflecting positively on the concept of organ donation and transplantation.

Decisions about organ donation and transplantation are left to individuals, but there are many references which support the concept of organ donation in Hindu scriptures.

In the list of ten niyamas (or virtuous acts) in the Hindu scriptures, daan (or selfless giving) is third and is held as being significant in the Hindu faith. That could also be seen as supporting the idea of organ donation. The only constraint on the idea of organ donation is imposed by the nature of dharma (righteous living). Every act or intention of anyone should be dharmik. It is right, therefore to donate organs only if the act of donating an organ has beneficial results.

There are no rules in Buddhism for or against organ donation, but central to Buddhism is a wish to relieve suffering. For the followers of this religion, donation depends on an individual's decision.

The death process of an individual is viewed as very important and, as such, the body should be treated with respect. However, there are no beliefs that say the body should be preserved in its entirety, so removing organs is not an issue from this point of view.

Organ Donation and Consciousness

A dead body should only be disturbed for appropriate reasons and with special care, however. It is also important to consider the consciousness of the dead person and whether this might

Ethnicities on the U.S. Organ Waiting List								
	All Organs	Kidney	Liver	Pancreas	Kidney/ Pancreas	Heart	Lung	Heart/ Lung	Intestine
All Ethnicities	107,201	81,338	16,761	1,609	2,342	2,672	2,149	94	236
White	50,354	31,712	11,891	1,326	1,541	1,925	1,749	60	150
Black	30,723	28,260	1,136	147	440	474	215	12	39
Hispanic	17,673	14,168	2,735	103	276	208	126	16	41
Unknown	3	0	2	0	0	1	0	0	0
Asian	6,385	5,443	803	20	35	38	37	4	5
American Indian/Alaska Native	1,024	872	98	6	28	10	9	1	0
Pacific Islander	514	464	26	3	12	5	4	0	0
Multiracial	525	419	70	4	10	11	9	1	1

TAKEN FROM: The Organ Procurement and Transplantation Network, data as of August 22, 2008.

be adversely affected by organ donation, as the surgery takes place immediately after the donor takes his or her last breath.

Some Buddhists, including those who follow Tibetan Buddhism, believe the consciousness may stay in the body for some time after breathing has stopped. Until the consciousness leaves the body it is important that it remains undisturbed, so Tibetan Buddhists might be concerned that an operation so soon after death will damage a person's consciousness and cause harm to their future lives. Others might decide this final act of generosity can only have positive results.

Judaism Permits Organ Donation

In principle, Judaism supports and encourages organ donation to save lives (pikuach nefesh). This principle can sometimes override the strong objections to any unnecessary interference with the body after death (nivul hamet) and the requirement for immediate burial of the complete body.

As all cases are different, Jewish law requires consultation with a competent rabbinic authority before consent is granted.

If an organ is needed for a specific, immediate transplant, it could be considered a great honour for a Jew to donate organs to save another person's life. But if the organs are donated into an organ bank, or for medical research, this might be looked on less favourably.

There is also concern that during the harvesting operation, the doctor might remove organs before the patient is actually dead according to Jewish law. This could be seen as effectively killing the patient, which is obviously forbidden.

Muslims May Donate Organs

Although organ donation and transplants are less common in Muslim countries, the UK Muslim Law (Shariah) Council released a fatwa (a religious opinion) in 1996 stating it was acceptable for Muslims to donate organs after their death and to accept organs if they need them.

Normally, violating a human body—whether living or dead—is outlawed in Islam, but the fatwa is based on the principle of necessity overruling prohibition, or al-daruart tubih al-mahzurat.

The council decided that:

- Organ transplantation is supported as a means of alleviating pain or saving life on the basis of the rules of the shariah.

- Muslims may carry donor cards.

- The next of kin of a dead person may give permission to obtain organs from the body to save other people's lives in the absence of a donor card or an expressed wish to donate organs.

Educating People About Organ Donation

For Ms. Davis, educating people in respect of their religious and moral fears boils down to funding. If there were 100 people doing a job like mine, we could say to religious leaders that this is our strategy, this is how it works, this is how we get out into the communities, this is what we do and then we can start to make an impact.

'But if there is not the funding for that, it is difficult to do. As far as I know, I am the only person who does this kind of work around organ donations,' she says.

Many people refuse permission for organ donation because they have never discussed it with their families or close ones. With such a shortfall among the minority ethnic population for organ transplants, it is increasingly important to raise awareness of the need for more black and Asian donors. One vital aspect in all of this is the cooperation of religious leaders.

Periodical Bibliography

The following articles have been selected to supplement the diverse views presented in this chapter.

American Society of Transplantation — "Who Can Be an Organ Donor?" December 2006.

T. Randolph Beard, John D. Jackson, and David L. Kaserman — "The Failure of U.S. Organ Procurement Policy," *Regulation*, Winter 2007.

Dan Davis — "The Ethics of Organ Allocation," *President's Council on Bioethics Staff Working and Discussion Paper*, September 7, 2006.

Haren Fanning — "Rescue Mission," *Scholastic Choices*, February-March 2005.

David L. Kaserman — "Fifty Years of Organ Transplants: The Successes and the Failures," *Issues in Law & Medicine*, Summer 2007.

Laura Meckler — "More Kidneys for Transplants May Go to Young," *The Wall Street Journal*, March 10, 2007.

Sally Satel — "Supply, Demand, and Kidney Transplants," *Policy Review*, August-September 2007.

Rob Stein — "A Third of Patients on Transplant List Are Not Eligible," *The Washington Post*, March 22, 2008.

Tracy Weber and Charles Ornstein — "4 More California Transplant Programs Under Scrutiny," *Los Angeles Times*, November 14, 2006.

Ben Whitford — "Who Gets the Organs?" *Newsweek*, November 28, 2005.

Todd Zwillich — "USA Confronts Looming Organ-Shortage Crisis," *The Lancet*, August 12, 2006.

OPPOSING
VIEWPOINTS®
SERIES

CHAPTER 2

How Can Organ Donation Be Increased?

Chapter Preface

A number of solutions have been debated for increasing the number of organ donations in the United States. One of the approaches that is discussed in this chapter is the creation of an organ market, where donors or their families receive compensation for donating an organ. Although an organ market does not exist in the United States, one has been in place in Iran since 1988. The success—and failure—of the Iranian organ market has been the subject of considerable debate.

The Iranian organ market was established in 1988. Potential recipients are not referred to the program unless they cannot receive a kidney from a living relative. The Dialysis and Transplant Patients Association, an independent agency, locates matching donors. Only unrelated donors are eligible for payment, receiving $1,200 and limited health care coverage from the government and additional money from the recipient (or charities if the recipient cannot afford payment), of approximately $3,000. According to Benjamin E. Hippen, in his report "Organ Sales and Moral Travails: Lessons from the Living Kidney Vendor Program in Iran," Iran eliminated the waiting list for kidneys in 1999. By comparison, the waiting list in the United States is 73,000 people.

The Iranian program has received considerable praise from Western analysts, who argue that the legalized organ market has virtually eliminated the organ shortage in Iran. The magazine *The Economist* contends, "Although there is little information on how donors ultimately fare, Iran can claim to have solved a problem which in most Western countries is growing more acute: a rapid increase in the number of people whose lives could be extended, or improved in quality, by kidney transplants." Kerry Howley, writing for *Reason* magazine, points out that donations by deceased donors—which are not entitled to payment—has grown steadily, indicating that altruistic donation is not in danger of vanishing when a regulated organ market is established.

Not everyone offers such effusive praise of the Iranian approach, however. An article in the *British Medical Journal* states that the waiting list for a kidney has not been completely eliminated, despite claims made by the program's supporters, and that many of the donors are still struggling financially and have developed health problems. Hippen acknowledges that insufficient information is available on the long-term health of organ donors and that such concerns are valid, though as a whole he believes the United States should not reject adopting a similar program.

The organ market that has been in place in Iran for twenty years is one way to respond to the shortage of donated organs. The authors in this chapter debate several potential solutions.

> "Markets in organs are the best available way to enable persons with defective organs to get transplants much more quickly than under the present system."

Allowing the Sale of Organs Will Increase the Number of Donations

Gary Becker

In the following viewpoint, Gary Becker contends that the shortage of available donor organs could be lessened if people were permitted to buy and sell organs on the open market. Becker asserts that an open market would not exploit the poor or people with short-term financial needs. According to Becker, criticisms of an organ market have been influenced largely by arguments about blood donation that are neither valid nor relevant. Becker is a professor of economics at the University of Chicago and a Nobel Prize winner.

As you read, consider the following questions:

1. According to Becker, approximately how many people died in 2000 while waiting for a kidney transplant?

Gary Becker, "Should the Purchase and Sales of Organs for Transplant Surgery Be Permitted?" *The Becker-Posner Blog*, January 1, 2006. Reproduced by permission of the author.

2. How much does a liver transplant cost, according to the author?

3. What book does Becker say has influenced arguments against the selling of organs?

There were about 50,000 persons on the waiting list for kidney transplants in the United States in the year 2000, but only about 15,000 kidney transplant operations were performed. This implies an average wait of almost four years before a person on the waiting list could receive a kidney transplant. The cumulative gap between demand and supply for livers was over 10,000, which implies an average wait for a liver transplant of a couple of years.

In 2000, almost 3,000 persons died while waiting for a kidney transplant, and half that number died while waiting for a liver transplant. Many also died in other countries while on the queue waiting for an organ transplant. Some of these people would have died anyway from other causes, but there is little doubt that most died too early because they were unable to replace their defective organs quickly enough.

Demand for Organs Outpaces Supply

If altruism were sufficiently powerful, the supply of organs would be large enough to satisfy demand, and there would be no need to change the present system. But this is not the case in any country that does a significant number of transplants. While the per capita number of organs donated has grown over time, demand has grown even faster. As a result, the length of the queue for organ transplants has grown significantly over time in most countries, despite exhortations and other attempts to encourage greater giving of organs.

In recent years the US [United States] has taken several steps to improve the allocation of available organs among those needing them, such as giving greater priority to those who could benefit the most. These steps have helped, but they have not stopped the queues from growing, nor prevented large numbers of persons from dying while waiting for transplants. Some countries use an "opt out" system for organs, which means that cadaveric organs can be used for transplants unless persons who died had indicated that they did not want their organs to be so used. A PhD thesis in progress by Sebastien Gay at [the University of] Chicago shows that opt out systems may yield somewhat more organs for transplants than the "opt in" systems used by the US and many other nations, but they do not eliminate the long queues for transplants.

To an economist, the major reason for the imbalance between demand and supply of organs is that the United States and practically all other countries forbid the purchase and sale of organs. This means that under present laws, people give their organs to be used after they die, or with kidneys and livers also while they are alive, only out of altruism and similar motives. In fact, practically all transplants of kidneys and livers with live donors are from one family member to another member. With live liver transplants, only a portion of the liver of a donor is used, and this grows over time in the donee, while the remaining portion regenerates over time in the donor.

A Free Market Would Increase the Organ Supply

If laws were changed so that organs could be purchased and sold, some people would give not out of altruism, but for the financial gain. The result would be an increased supply of organs. In a free market, the prices of organs for transplants would settle at the levels that would eliminate the excess demand for each type of organ. In a paper on the potential of markets for live organ donations, Julio Elias of the University of Buffalo and I estimate that the going price for live transplants would be about $15,000 for kidneys and about $35,000 for livers. We recognize, however, that the data are too limited to be confident that these numbers would be close to equilibrium prices that equate supply and demand—they may be too high or too low. But even if our estimates were only half the actual equilibrium prices, the effect on the total cost of transplants would not be huge since current costs for live transplants in the US are in the range of $100,000 for kidney transplants and $175,000 for liver transplants.

An open market in organs would sharply curtail the present black market where some persons in need of transplants have them in poorer countries like Turkey where enforcement against selling organs is slack. Since the quality of the surgeons and hospitals in these countries is much lower than in advanced countries, this often greatly reduces the quality of the organs used and how well they are matched to the organ types of recipients.

Still, despite these strong arguments in favor of allowing commercial markets in organs, I do not expect such markets to be permitted any time in the near future because the opposition is fierce. Some critics simply dismiss organ markets as immoral "commodification" of body parts. More thoughtful critics suggest that allowing organs to be bought and sold might actually reduce the total number of organs available for transplants because they claim it would sufficiently lower the number of organs donated from altruistic motives to dominate the increase due to those sold commercially. That scenario, however, is extremely unlikely since presently only a small fraction of potentially useable organs are available for transplants. Compensating persons either for allowing their organs to be used after their death, or for kidneys and livers to be used while they are alive, would enormously widen the scope of the potential organ market.

An Organ Market Would Not Harm the Poor

Another set of critics agree with me that the effect on the total supply of organs from allowing them to be purchased and sold would be large and positive, but they object to markets

A Parallel to Medical Research

The strongest parallel [to an organ market] can be drawn with payments to volunteer participants in research studies. Without payment, it is unlikely that sufficient people would volunteer. Solicitations are openly advertised and condoned by regulatory bodies responsible for the supervision of human investigations. The same university newspaper that carried the advertisement for egg donors contained twenty-three advertisements for study participants, ranging from healthy adults to smokers, obese people, and even children younger than three years old. Although most of these research protocols entail safe interventions, any investigation conducted to advance medicine and science may result in unexpected and even catastrophic events. . . . If it is reasonable, legal, and ethically justified to motivate someone using monetary reward to participate in human research, then by extension the same person should be allowed a monetary inducement or reward for donating an organ.

Amy L. Friedman, "Payment for Living Organ Donation Should Be Legalised," British Medical Journal, *October 7, 2006.*

because of a belief that the commercially-motivated part of the organ supply would mainly come from the poor. In effect, they believe the poor would be induced to sell their organs to the middle classes and the rich. It is hard to see any reasons to complain if organs of poor persons were sold with their permission after they died, and the proceeds went as bequests to their parents or children. The complaints would be louder if, for example, mainly poor persons sold one of their kidneys for live kidney transplants, but why would poor donors be better off if this option were taken away from them? If so desired, a quota could be placed on the fraction of organs that could be supplied by persons with incomes below a certain level, but would that improve the welfare of poor persons?

Moreover, it is far from certain that a dominant fraction of the organs would come from the poor in a free market. Many of the organs used for live liver or kidney transplants are still likely to be supplied by relatives. In addition, many middle class persons would be willing to have their organs sold after they died if the proceeds went to children, parents, and other relatives. Although this is not an exact analogy, predictions that a voluntary army would be filled mainly with poor persons have turned out to be wrong. Many of the poor do not have the education and other qualifications to be acceptable to the armed forces. In the same way, many poor persons in the US would have organs that would not be acceptable in a market system because of organ damage due to drug use or various diseases.

Still another criticism of markets in organs is that people would be kidnapped for their organs, and that totalitarian governments would sell organs of prisoners. This would happen, but not likely on a significant scale since the source of organs offered for sale could be determined in most cases without great difficulty.

A criticism particularly of a commercial market for live transplants is that some persons would act impulsively out of short run financial needs, and that they would regret their decision to sell a kidney or allow their liver to be used for a transplant if they had taken more time. I do not know how important such impulsive behavior would be, but it could be sharply reduced by having a month or longer cooling off waiting period between the time someone agrees to supply an organ and the time it can be used. They would be allowed to change their mind during the interim.

Parallels with the Blood Market

Many of the arguments against the sale of organs indirectly stem from an influential book in 1971 by the British social scientist Richard Titmuss, *The Gift Relationship: From Human Blood to Social Policy*. He argues against allowing blood to be sold for transfusions, and compares the British system, which did not allow the purchase of blood, with the American system, which did allow its purchase. Titmuss basically ignored that the American system in fact was getting more blood per capita than the British system. Instead, he concentrated on the quality of the blood. Since a significant fraction of the American blood came from individuals with hepatitis and other diseases that could not be screened out, the blood given under the British system tended to be healthier. In the absence of effective screening techniques, perhaps shutting down the commercial market was an effective way then to improve blood quality.

But that is no longer the case as highly effective methods have since been developed to determine whether blood is contaminated with various types of hepatitis, the HIV virus, and other transmittable diseases. Under present screening technology, a market in blood yields much more blood, and with enough diligence its quality can be maintained at a high level.

My conclusion is that markets in organs are the best available way to enable persons with defective organs to get transplants much more quickly than under the present system. I do not find compelling the arguments against allowing the sale of organs, especially when weighed against the number of lives that would be saved by the increased supply stimulated by financial incentives.

| "Are we ready to live with a system that
makes kidneys a commodity?"

Allowing the Sale of Organs Could Cause Serious Problems

Sheila M. Rothman and David J. Rothman

In the following viewpoint, Sheila M. Rothman and David J. Rothman argue that permitting the sale of organs would create ethical problems and fail to benefit organ sellers. The authors assert that if selling organs became legal, people facing significant financial problems might feel pressured to pursue that option; however, studies have shown that the financial benefits may be short lived. In addition, they argue, an organ market would be difficult to regulate and could create unexpected problems. Sheila M. Rothman is a professor of public health at the Joseph L. Mailman School of Public Health at Columbia University. David J. Rothman is director of the Center for the Study of Society and Medicine at the Columbia College of Physicians and Surgeons.

As you read, consider the following questions:

1. As explained by the authors, how were the number of late pickups at an Israeli day care center affected when a fine was imposed?

Sheila M. Rothman and David J. Rothman, "The Hidden Cost of Organ Sale," *American Journal of Transplantation*, vol. 6, July 2006, pp. 1524–1528. Copyright © 2006 Basil Blackwell Ltd. Reproduced by permission of Blackwell Publishers.

2. What figure do the authors suggest as a potential price for a kidney?

3. According to a study cited by the authors, what percentage of kidney sellers in India still had debt six years later?

The idea of establishing a market for organs, although certainly not new, is now attracting unprecedented support. Much of the enthusiasm comes from members of the transplant community, but it is also favored by a growing number of economists and bioethicists who believe that the sale of body parts has become 'morally imperative'. To be sure, the practice is explicitly prohibited by U.S. law, rejected by the guidelines of almost every national and international transplant society and opposed by many commentators. But never before has a market solution been so vigorously endorsed.

Almost every article advocating legalization opens by noting the shortfall in organs (over 50,000 people await a kidney), and the resulting increase in morbidity and mortality. At the same time, the number of living donors has increased dramatically (they now provide more than half of all kidneys for transplantation), to the benefit of recipients and apparently without harm to themselves. Thus, as one transplant surgeon has observed: 'Discussing organ sales simply does not feel right, but letting candidates die on the waiting list (when this could be prevented) does not feel right either.'

Ethics has occupied a central place in the debate over the sale of kidneys, with two key principles vying for primacy. Proponents emphasize the concept of autonomy—the right of persons to sell their body parts, free of heavy-handed paternalism. Opponents invoke standards of fairness and justice; the poor will sell their kidneys to the rich, engendering systematic exploitation. What has been relegated to the margins, however, is full consideration of the implications of such a system for medicine and for society. Proponents flatly assert that sale would increase the supply and not reduce the rate of altruistic donation. They posit that such a market could be effectively regulated and that sellers would benefit greatly from the financial windfall. But these claims are not well substantiated and may prove wrong. No less important, they fail to take into account the many other possible effects of allowing a market in organs.

Because the intended and unintended consequences of policy change cannot be easily predicted, this analysis is put forward in tentative, even speculative, terms. The aim is to raise considerations that may have been glossed over, to highlight the possibilities that have not been imagined, and to prompt second thoughts about postulates that seem obvious. The intent is not to persuade one side or the other that these projections will inevitably be realized but to encourage both sides to deepen and widen the scope of their concerns. Just as studies of the possible impact of legislation on the environment are mandated, so the likely impact of legalization of organ sale warrants consideration.

Cash Payments Affect Moral Obligations

Advocates think it self-evident that market incentives will yield more organs for transplantation. 'People are more likely to do something if they are going to get paid for it.' And sellers will not drive out donors. Whatever financial incentives exist, siblings and parents will continue to donate to loved ones.

These expectations, however, may be disappointed. Since the 1970s, a group of economists and social psychologists have been analyzing the tensions between 'extrinsic incentives'—financial compensation and monetary rewards, and 'intrinsic incentives'—the moral commitment to do one's duty. They hypothesize that extrinsic incentives can 'crowd out' intrinsic incentives, that the introduction of cash payments will weaken moral obligations. As Uri Gneezy, a professor of behavioral science at the University of Chicago School of Business, observes: 'Extrinsic motivation might change the perception of the activity and destroy the intrinsic motivation to perform it when no apparent reward apart from the activity itself is expected.' Although the case for the 'hidden costs of rewards' is certainly not indisputable, it does suggest that a market in organs might reduce altruistic donation and overall supply.

Perhaps the most celebrated analysis of the tension between intrinsic and extrinsic incentives is [Richard] Titmuss' work in blood donation. His book, *The Gift Relationship*, argued that the 'commercialization of blood represses the expression of altruism (and) erodes the sense of community.' Payment undermined the altruistic motivations of would-be blood donors. Titmuss supported his hypothesis by comparing blood donation in the United States and the United Kingdom. Analyzing data from England and Wales over the period 1946–1968, where the sale of blood was prohibited, Titmuss found that the percentage of the population who donated blood and the amount of blood donated steadily increased. By comparison, in the United States, where the sale of blood was allowed, donations declined. Because U.S. data were more fragmentary, Titmuss drew as best he could on a variety of sources, including surveys, municipal statistics and comments by medical experts and blood bank officials. Nevertheless, he confidently concluded: The data, 'when analyzed in microscopic fashion, blood bank by blood bank, area by area, city by city, state by state', revealed 'a generally worsening situation'.

Following Titmuss's lead, other studies have tried to buttress the empirical case for crowding out. One intriguing experiment turned an Israeli day care center into a research site. It was not unusual for some parents to arrive late to pick up their children; center administrators complained but levied no penalties. The researchers first took a baseline measure of the frequency of lateness and then had the center post a notice on its bulletin board: 'The official closing time . . . is 1600. Since some parents have been coming late, we ... have decided to impose a fine. ... NIS 10 ($2.50) will be charged every time a child is collected after 1610. The fine will be calculated monthly, and is to be paid with the regular monthly payment'. Although one might have predicted that late pickups would decline, the number actually increased. And even when several weeks later the researchers had the center cancel the late charge, the higher level of lateness persisted.

To explain these outcomes, the researchers proposed that in the pre-fine days, parents interpreted the extra time that the teacher spent taking care of the children as 'a generous, nonmarket activity'; they did their best to arrive on time because the teacher was considerate and should 'not be taken advantage of'. Once the fine was levied, the added time of child care had a price and parents believed they could purchase it as often as necessary. 'When help is offered for no compensation in a moment of need, accept it with restraint. When a service is offered for a price, buy as much as you find convenient'. Moreover, the lateness persisted after the elimination of the charge because there was no reverting to the older norm once the charge had been levied: 'Once a commodity, always a commodity'. ...

Social and Economic Consequences

What impact might organ sale have on day-to-day social interactions? Let us make a few preliminary assumptions. The purchase price for an organ would have to be nontrivial. One calculation, based on cost savings were transplantation to more completely replace dialysis, sets the figure at $275 000 per kidney. For sake of argument, let us divide that number by a little more than half and use a price of $125 000. Because government policy would have to strongly favor such an arrangement, let us also presume that the sum would be tax free.

Would sellers be attracted? Undoubtedly. They would likely come from the lower class and lower-middle class, although at this price some in the middle class might participate as well. It is doubtful that anyone with significant means would sell a kidney even for a substantial sum.

The removal of the kidney would leave an indelible mark in the form of a scar. Were the procedure done laparoscopically, it would be small and not easily distinguished from other surgical interventions. Still, it would be visible, if not to strangers then to intimates. Evidence of the sale would thus be written on the body and speak to moral character. It would point not to heroism and generosity of spirit (intrinsic reward) but to desperation and avariciousness (extrinsic reward). In fact, a study conducted in Iran found that kidney sellers suffered extreme shame in their community. In the United States, the opprobrium might be even greater. Historians of punishment, for example, have proposed that the practice of public torture was abandoned in the 18th century not because the punishments were ineffective, but because citizens shared new and acute sensibilities about bodily integrity, which the spectacle of dismemberment violated. Although a surgical scar does not rise to this level, it may still be asked whether we are ready to countenance the signs of kidney sale.

The everyday consequences of an organ market might create other problems. If kidney sale brought a payment of $125 000 tax free, it would make financial sense to undergo the procedure sooner rather than later. For someone at age 21, investing $125 000, perhaps in a mutual fund, would likely double the sum by age 30. Should one then boast of the sale to a prospective partner? At what point in a relationship would one relate the fact? Would it be presented as having the means for a down payment on a starter home? Would the partner be obliged to sell a kidney in the future to enable a move to a still larger home? Should one anticipate inquiries from prospective in-laws on whether you have yet sold your kidney?

Selling Organs Can Lead to Health Problems

In India, about 2,000 people sell a kidney each year. One study there in 2002 found 86 percent of organ sellers saying they had significant declines in their health in the three years after surgery. In the eastern European nation of Moldova, some 300 peasants sold their kidneys between 1999 and 2002. A study by Organs Watch found 79 percent of Moldovan donors with health problems in the months and years after the procedure.

Abraham McLaughlin et al., "What's a Kidney Worth?"
Christian Science Monitor, *June 9, 2004.*

Should one anticipate such questions from bill collectors (in India this is not hypothetical), or from welfare or unemployment officers or from attorneys in bankruptcy proceedings? Should one also anticipate parents asking an 18-year-old to sell a kidney to offset substantial college tuition costs, or later, wedding costs?

In sum, the implications for social relationships of transforming body parts into commodities are unknown and might bring unintended negative consequences. As Margret Radin, a professor of law, has astutely observed: 'The law both expresses and works to form and evolve cultural characteristics and commitments. . . . "Preferences" bring law into being, but law also makes and changes "preferences"'. Because there is feedback between law and culture, we might come to regret the legalization of kidney sale.

The Myth of the Regulated Market

Proponents offer very different models for a market in organs, making it difficult to know precisely what is being advocated. Some would restrict compensation to cadaveric organs and give credits to families who agree to the removal. Others, including a committee of the American Medical Association, endorse a futures market in organs: they would compensate would-be donors for agreeing to organ removal upon death. Still others urge a regulated market among living vendors but provide almost no details. Mostly everyone rejects a public auction with the kidney going to the highest bidder; the preference is for distribution by a central, UNOS-like organization, permitting individuals to sell but not to purchase an organ. Such compromises, it should be noted, are inconsistent with proponents' attachment to the market. After all, people are even more likely to do something if they are very well paid for it—so why not permit auctions?

Whatever the proposed system, regulation may not be readily accomplished. Once a market is lawful, half-way measures that allow for sellers but not for buyers might prove inoperative. Effectively regulated markets typically involve so-called 'natural monopolies' wherein entry points can be effectively policed. (Think of electric power, telephone service, and railroads.) By contrast, in kidney sale, with almost everyone eligible to enter the market, oversight will not be easily established or maintained. So too, as most students of regulated markets are quick to admit, change almost inevitably carries unintended consequences. Deregulate the market in energy trading and Enron scandals occur; deregulate the telephone market and the communications industry is transformed; deregulate the savings and loan business and corruption breaks out. Hence, the question must be asked: since practices may develop in ways that cannot be predicted or controlled, are we ready to live with a system that makes kidneys a commodity? . . .

Kidney Sales May Not Benefit the Poor

One claim frequently made to justify kidney markets is that the sums paid to vendors will redound [contribute] to their economic benefit. The bioethicist Robert Veatch recently retracted his long-held opposition to sale, arguing that because American society has so neglected the poor, objections must be put aside. Social welfare programs are so inadequate that it is wrong to oppose a measure that might assist them. The empirical question, however, is whether organ sale would actually benefit the poor or, to the contrary, bring even more deleterious effects.

The best data comes from the third world. In India, as [Madhav] Goyal et al. have documented, 87 percent of kidney sellers reported a deterioration of health status and one third, a decrease in family income. Of 292 persons who sold a kidney to pay off debts, 74 percent still had debts 6 years later, and those in poverty increased from 54 percent prior to the sale to 71 percent after the sale. These findings are reinforced by [Lawrence] Cohen's in-depth interviews with 30 sellers and their families in Madras [India]. Although they were attempting to pay off debts, he found that 'sellers are frequently back in debt in a few years'. He also discovered that debt collectors became more aggressive in 'kidney selling zones', making a system of sale self-reinforcing.

To be sure, the American experience might be different, with the economic returns from sale promoting property mobility. But kidney sale might also have a negative impact on social welfare policy. Some proponents have argued, for example, that kidney sellers should receive lifetime health insurance, and in this way move the country closer to national health insurance. But legalized kidney sale might have the very opposite effect. If you want health insurance, sell your organ. Surely this is not the most promising method for accomplishing a more just distribution of health care benefits. Were there no organ shortage, no one would propose kidney sale as a way of equalizing economic conditions.

However lamentable the consequences of the shortage of organs, kidney sale might turn out to be counterproductive. It might not produce the increase in organs that proponents anticipate. More, it might engender conditions inimical to professional medical practice and social cohesion.

> "A paired exchange can save two lives and remove two people from the [Organ Procurement and Transplantation Network] waiting list, freeing up two future organs to be given to other people."

Paired Donations Will Increase the Organ Supply

David J. Undis

The organ shortage crisis can be lessened through the use of paired and intended recipient organ exchanges, argues David J. Undis in the following viewpoint. As Undis explains, these exchanges enable potential recipients to find live organ donors, even if they do not have family or friends who are medically compatible. According to Undis, people who avoid the organ allocation system by utilizing these exchanges are freeing up organs for people who must remain on the organ waiting list. Undis is executive director of LifeSharers, a nonprofit national network of organ donors.

David J. Undis, "Escaping the System: The Current System of Organ Allocation and the Attempts to Survive It," *Speech to Albany Medical College's "Health, Care and Society" class*, March 15, 2006. Reproduced by permission.

As you read, consider the following questions:

1. According to Undis, what are the four objectives of organ allocation policies?

2. By how much did the number of living donors increase between 1988 and 2005, according to the author?

3. As stated by Undis, what percentage of Americans are registered organ donors?

Today I'm going to describe the organ allocation system and some of the attempts to circumvent it. But if I had been given a chance to write the title for today's session, it would have been: "Escaping the System: The Current System of Organ Allocation and the Attempts to Survive It." People aren't trying to game the system. They're trying to escape it. People aren't attempting to circumvent the system. They're attempting to survive it.

Before looking at the organ allocation system itself, let's look at why people are trying to escape it. The reason is simple—if they don't escape the system, the system will probably kill them.

A "Waiting To Die" List

In June of 2003, Dr. Robert Metzger testified before Congress during hearings titled "Assessing Initiatives to Increase Organ Donations." At the time, Dr. Metzger was President-Elect of the United Network for Organ Sharing [UNOS]. UNOS is a private organization that operates the national organ allocation system under a contract with the federal government. Here's part of what Dr. Metzger had to say:

"Over 81,000 patients are on the wait-list for transplantation in the United States today and more than 5,000 will die this year without receiving a transplant. More startling is that almost 60 percent of those on the list today will die without receiving a transplant."

That was 33 months ago. The transplant waiting list has grown since then. . . . Today, the list contains over 91,000 names, not 81,000. So if Dr. Metzger was testifying today, he wouldn't be saying that almost 60 percent of those on the list today will die without receiving a transplant. He'd be saying that over 60 percent will die.

Two weeks before his testimony, in an interview with a Florida newspaper, Dr. Metzger called the transplant waiting list "the waiting to die list."

Is it any wonder that people who need transplants are "circumventing" the organ allocation system? If your mother, your sister, or your daughter needed a transplant, would you suggest that she submit to a system that will probably let her die? I doubt it. No, I think you would help her find ways to save her life.

Before we look at some of the ways to do that, let's examine the organ allocation system.

The Laws Behind Organ Donation

I am not a doctor. It is not my intent . . . to go into technical medical matters here. Rather, I want to explain the legal foundation and the goals of the system.

State law covers the mechanics of organ donation—how to make an anatomical gift, how to revoke one, and things like that. But our organ allocation system has its roots in federal law, specifically in the National Organ Transplant Act of 1984.

That law established the Organ Procurement and Transplantation Network [OPTN]. The OPTN is charged with maintaining a national list of individuals who need organs. It is also charged with maintaining a system for allocating available organs to individuals on that list.

The National Organ Transplant Act also made it illegal to pay for organs to be used in transplant operations. In my opinion, this is the real source of the organ shortage. The government made it illegal to buy or sell organs, so that the only supply of organs is donated organs. If the government did the same thing with food and shoes, we'd have a whole lot of hungry barefoot people.

Under the National Organ Transplant Act, operation of the OPTN is contracted to a private entity. Since 1986, the United Network for Organ Sharing has held that contract and operated the OPTN. For purposes of [this viewpoint], OPTN and UNOS are essentially interchangeable.

The Secretary of the Department of Health and Human Services has authority over OPTN, and he wields a big stick. Under the Social Security Act of 1986, hospitals that have transplant programs are required to follow OPTN rules and regulations. If they don't, their entire operations—not just their transplant operations—are disqualified from participating in Medicare and Medicaid. So hospitals don't mess with OPTN rules.

OPTN Allocation Rules

The OPTN issued a "Final Rule" in 1999. It lays out how organ allocation policies are to be developed. The purpose of the final rule is "to help achieve the most equitable and medically effective use of human organs that are donated in trust for transplantation." Keep this in mind as we go along today: equity and medical effectiveness are the overriding goals to be achieved in developing organ allocation policies.

It's also important to keep in mind that OPTN allocation policies only apply to organs from deceased donors. They do not apply to organs from live donors.

OPTN's Board of Directors is charged with developing these policies. Under the Final Rule, about 50 percent of the members of the OPTN board must be transplant surgeons or transplant physicians, and at least 25 percent of the members must be transplant candidates, transplant recipients, organ donors, and family members. The board must also include representatives of organ procurement organizations, transplant hospitals, voluntary health associations, transplant coordinators, histocompatibility experts, nonphysician transplant professionals, and the general public.

The Policies Behind Organ Allocation

Let's look at some of the requirements for developing policies for allocating organs from deceased donors.

First, organ allocation policies shall be based on sound medical judgment. It's hard to argue with that one.

Second, allocation policies shall seek to achieve the best use of donated organs. That sounds good, too.

Third, organ allocation policies should be different for different organs. That makes sense.

Next, organ allocation policies shall be designed to achieve four different objectives: don't waste organs, don't perform futile transplants, promote patient access to transplants, and promote efficient organ placement. This is all good.

Next, the organ allocation system is to be a national system, not a series of local or regional ones, unless that conflicts with the requirements we've already mentioned.

Finally, organ allocation policies cannot prohibit directed donation, which means they can't stop organ donors from donating to specific individuals of their choosing. Directed donation is also legal under the laws of all 50 states and the District of Columbia.

This is a good time to point out that the organ allocation system in the United States is really two systems. The first system is the OPTN system I've just described. It applies to organs that are "donated in trust for transplantation." When people talk about "the organ allocation system" this is the system they're talking about. But there is a second system, the directed donation system. It applies to organs that are not donated "in trust" but are donated to specific individuals. As we shall see, this second system is playing an increasingly important role in allocating organs.

Paired Donations Should Be a National Program

It is critical to the success and public perception of KPD [kidney paired donation] that careful consideration be given to what impact a local/regional vs. national scheme will have on the ability to make transplants available to the greatest number of patients both equitably and cost-efficiently. Determining optimal allocation priorities and algorithms is absolutely crucial to the smart proliferation of KPD in the United States and the prevention of a haphazard system that diminishes the impact of this promising approach to the organ shortage. . . .

An optimized national KPD scheme would result in significant rewards for those who are willing to travel, as well as for the remaining pool of patients. Furthermore, only 2.9 percent of the donor/recipient pairs would actually need to travel to achieve the maximum benefit from an optimized algorithm. This finding discredits one of the most widely perceived barriers to implementation of a national KPD program and greatly reduces the need to transport patients or organs between regions.

Dorry L. Segev, et al.,
Journal of the American Medical Association,
April 20, 2005.

Two Problems with the Allocation System

So that's how policies for allocating organs from deceased donors are to be developed. None of this seems controversial. Of course, the devil is in the details. We're not going to go there, except to point out two things.

First, there's lots of room in these guidelines for interpretation and value judgments. For example, what exactly is "the most equitable use of donated organs?" What is "the most medically effective use of donated organs?" What is "the best use of donated organs?" All of these terms are used in OPTN's policy development guidelines. What is "sound medical judgment?" And what is a "futile transplant?" Reasonable people can, and do, disagree on all these questions.

Second, because these guidelines have more than one goal, it's almost impossible to avoid conflict. Recall the overriding goals: "the most equitable and medically effective use" of donated organs. Even if everyone agreed on what those two things mean, it's by no means clear that what is most medically effective is most equitable, or that what is most equitable is most medically effective.

Family and Friend Donations Save Lives

Let's turn now to some of the ways people use to escape the OPTN organ allocation system.

Broadly speaking, the most common way of escaping the OPTN organ allocation system is through live organ donation. . . .

There were about 4 times as many living donors last year [2005] as in 1988. During that same period, the number of deceased donors grew only about 3.5 percent per year. About half of all organ donors are now live donors.

The overwhelming majority of live organ donors are kidney donors, and just about all of these donations are from family member to family member, or from friend to friend. For example, John Jones donates a kidney to Jane Jones, and Sam Smith donates a kidney to Sally Smith.

People who accept an organ from a family member or a friend are circumventing the OPTN organ allocation system. So are the people who donate them. Does that make live organ donation a bad thing? I don't think so. During the period covered on the previous chart, about 78,000 people received transplants from living donors. That's a lot of lives saved, and every time a person who receives a transplant from a live donor is removed from the OPTN waiting list that frees up an organ from a deceased donor to be given to someone else.

Paired and Intended Recipient Exchanges Are Beneficial

Let's return to our example. Not everyone who needs a kidney has a family member or a friend who is both willing to donate a kidney and who is medically compatible as a donor. So variations on the theme of live organ donation have arisen.

The first of these is called paired exchanges. Using our example, let's assume that John Jones is willing to donate a kidney to Jane Jones but John and Jane are not medically compatible. Likewise, assume Sam Smith is willing to donate a kidney to Sally Smith, but they aren't medically compatible. Well, if John Jones and Sally Smith are compatible, and if Jane Jones and Sam Smith are compatible, then they can make a swap. John Jones can donate a kidney to Sally Smith, and Sam Smith can donate a kidney to Jane Jones.

Paired exchanges also circumvent the OPTN organ allocation system. Is that a bad thing?

Again, I don't think so. A paired exchange can save two lives and remove two people from the OPTN waiting list, freeing up two future organs to be given to other people.

Another type of exchange is called the intended recipient exchange. Again using our example, let's assume John Jones is willing to donate a kidney to Jane Jones but they are not medically compatible. This time, let's assume they can't find anyone like the Smiths with whom they can arrange a swap. In an intended recipient exchange, John Jones donates his kidney and it is transplanted into someone who is on the

OPTN waiting list. In exchange, Jane Jones gets bumped up the OPTN waiting list and gets a kidney from a deceased donor sooner than she otherwise would have.

Here we have an interesting intersection between live organ donation and OPTN's system for allocating organs from deceased donors. You don't need OPTN's permission to donate a kidney to your sister. You don't need OPTN's permission to participate in a paired exchange. But you do need OPTN's permission and cooperation to arrange an intended recipient exchange.

Are intended recipient exchanges a good thing? I think so. In all likelihood, before he found out that his sister needed a kidney, John Jones had no intention of donating one of his. He only decided to donate when he found out his sister needed one. So intended recipient exchanges increase the supply of transplantable organs and save lives.

But there is some controversy with intended recipient exchanges. The Jane Joneses of the world tend to be the people who are hardest to match. They tend to wait the longest on the OPTN waiting list. The organ Jane gets through an intended recipient exchange probably would have otherwise gone to someone else who is hard to match and had been waiting a long time. So intended recipient exchanges may increase waiting times for some people on the OPTN waiting list. . . .

The Organ Allocation System Should Save Lives

Today, only about 40 percent of Americans are registered organ donors. Over the last 20 years, millions of millions of dollars have been spent by lots of wonderful organizations trying to make people aware of the need for more organ donors. These efforts have not been successful in reducing the organ shortage.

All of the alternatives to the OPTN allocation system we've discussed today are helping to reduce that shortage. All of them are legal, all of them are ethical, and all of them are helping save lives.

That should be the primary goal of the organ allocation system—to save as many lives as possible. OPTN and UNOS should not criticize or oppose efforts to save more lives. They should encourage and support them.

| "Paired and list donation are, some might argue, forms of organ trading."

Paired and List Donations Are the Wrong Way to Increase the Organ Supply

Sam Crowe

In the following viewpoint, Sam Crowe opines that paired and list donations—alternatives to the organ donation waiting list that enable incompatible donors and recipients to work together to make organs available—will not solve the organ shortage crisis. Crowe acknowledges that the Organ Procurement and Transplantation Network (OPTN) could implement paired and list donation into the organ allocation system. However, in his opinion, these forms of donation are ethically questionable and ultimately have a minimal positive impact on the supply of transplantable organs. Crowe is a policy analyst for the President's Council on Bioethics. The purpose of the council is to advise the administration on bioethical issues and to explore advances in biomedical science and technology.

As you read, consider the following questions:

1. What is a "chain exchange" organ donation, as explained by Crowe?

Sam Crowe, "Increasing the Supply of Human Organs: Three Policy Proposals," President's Council on Bioethics, February 2007.

2. According to the author, what is the ethical dilemma concerning people needing blood-type O kidneys?

3. As stated by Crowe, how many transplants resulted from paired and list donations?

As of January 18th, 2007, there were 94,664 Americans on the OPTN [Organ Procurement and Transplantation Network] transplant waiting list. Patients needing kidneys make up the largest group, accounting for roughly two-thirds of the list. By most projections, their numbers are likely to increase significantly in the next few decades. As Dr. Neil Powe explained to the Council [the President's Council on Bioethics] during the June 2006 meeting, we are seeing only the proverbial "tip of the iceberg" of chronic kidney disease: those Americans who have kidney failure make up only a very small percentage of those who have chronic kidney disease. But the large numbers of Americans who are today creeping toward kidney failure are only a part of the picture: during the next few decades the baby boomers will become elderly and thus more susceptible to kidney failure; public health experts are predicting a surge in diabetes, which is one of the main causes of kidney disease; and American minority populations, which tend to have higher rates of kidney disease than whites, are expected to increase substantially. If Dr. Powe's analysis is correct, America is on the verge of a massive increase in the demand for transplantable kidneys.

Solving the Demand for Kidneys

Some have argued that the best way to address organ failure is not by seeking to increase the supply of organs from deceased or living donors, but rather through other means, that is, by exploiting the potential of preventive medicine and regenerative medicine. The first would aim at improving the health of the population, and would thus shrink the number of individuals needing kidneys (or other organs) in the future, while the second would provide alternative treatments for organ failure, such as regenerating organs using stem cells. If these methods were to achieve the results envisioned by their advocates, we could look forward to an eventual end of the organ shortage—and of the burdens of morbidity that fuel it.

There is good reason, however, to doubt that these approaches will produce the desired results. As for regenerative medicine, despite the progress that has been made, for example, in generating structurally integrated bladder cells, this solution is for now more theory than reality and will not constitute an effective response to organ failure in the near future.

As for preventive medicine, if there were a well-established national program with considerable support from—and participation by—the American public, it could inhibit the growth in the need or demand for organs, but it, too, faces serious limitations. Although some causes of kidney disease are probably preventable through healthy practices such as a good diet, exercise, and sufficient sleep, preventive medicine cannot ultimately forestall the natural aging of the body. As human beings age, their kidneys lose the ability to function properly, so much so that if a person does not die by other causes that person will die from organ failure. With a graying America, this complication cannot be overlooked. Also, as every nutritionist and yoga instructor knows, being healthy is difficult. Many Americans will not follow the strict regimen of diet and exercise necessary to get and stay healthy, and even for those who change their ways, the disease processes set in motion by years and decades of sub-optimal health habits are often not readily reversible. In light of these constraints, we can expect only so much from preventive medicine. If our aim is to satisfy the current as well as future demand for replacement organs, we have no choice but to look, first and foremost, to ways of increasing the organ supply. . . .

Paired Donation and List Donation Explained

Paired donation and list donation are creative forms of organ giving, allowing living donors who are biologically incompatible with their intended recipients to work together with one another, or in conjunction with the public waiting list, to make donation possible in cases when otherwise it would not be. In paired donation, two biologically incompatible, living donor-recipient pairs—pair A and pair B—can surmount the biological barriers to donation in this way: donor A gives a kidney to biologically compatible recipient B and donor B gives a kidney to biologically compatible recipient A. Paired donations can occur between and among multiple pairs of donors and recipients. With list donation, a living donor who wishes to give a kidney to a biologically incompatible recipient donates the organ, instead, to the first individual in line on the waiting list for kidneys; in exchange, the living donor's intended recipient receives the next available compatible kidney or a higher place on the waiting list.

Paired donation and list donation can be combined and used together in a "chain exchange." Chain exchanges, in their simplest form, entail two pairs (A and B) that do not qualify for paired donation, meaning that both donors do not match the recipients of the opposite pair. Instead, only the donor of pair A matches the recipient of pair B. In a chain exchange, the donor of pair A gives a kidney to the intended recipient of pair B, and the donor of pair B in turn gives a kidney to the general kidney list. The intended recipient of pair A then moves up the waiting list for kidneys.

Paired donation and list donation are not new, untried ideas. Transplant surgeons in some centers have been matching donors and recipients and performing transplants in these ways for the past few years. In fact, there have been an estimated 62 list donations and 149 transplants using paired donations carried out in the United States. Nevertheless, the legal status of these forms of donation remains in question, and in February 2006 the Living Kidney Organ Donation Clarification Act was introduced in the Senate. The aim of this bill is to clarify that paired donation and list donation do not fall under the prohibition against "valuable consideration."

Establishing Protocols

Beyond clarifying the legality of these practices, there are two main ways that a policy promoting paired and list donation could be implemented. First, the OPTN could establish protocols for paired and list donation in a similar fashion as it has for the more conventional forms of donation. The OPTN would most likely create a national paired donation registry and clear rules to ensure that list donations do not unfairly disadvantage those who are already at the top of the waiting list, especially those with rare blood types. This approach would presumably bring many potential donors to the registry, and would unify the registry policy and living organ donation policy more generally.

The second approach would consist of providing federal assistance to improve the science and application of regionally-based paired donation and list donation programs. The federal assistance would be offered primarily to existing programs to subsidize patient registries, transplant coordinator salaries, education programs, and research and development. By offering assistance primarily to existing programs, this approach utilizes the expertise that the regionally-based paired and list donation programs already possess. In this way, federal funds are not wasted creating new programs when well-managed programs already exist.

If the Council wishes to lend its support to these forms of donation it could recommend passage by Congress of the Living Kidney Organ Donation Clarification Act or a similar bill, and encourage the creation of expanded and ethically responsible national/local protocols for paired donation and list do-

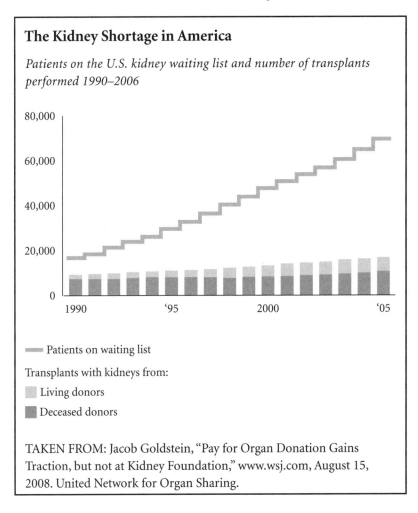

The Kidney Shortage in America

Patients on the U.S. kidney waiting list and number of transplants performed 1990–2006

— Patients on waiting list

Transplants with kidneys from:

Living donors

Deceased donors

TAKEN FROM: Jacob Goldstein, "Pay for Organ Donation Gains Traction, but not at Kidney Foundation," www.wsj.com, August 15, 2008. United Network for Organ Sharing.

nation. Passage of the Act would facilitate this creative form of donation, allowing generous potential donors to become actual donors. Through these measures, the bonds of community could be both widened and deepened, binding individuals to one another through mutual acts of generosity.

Paired and List Donations Are Ethically Questionable

Yet these forms of donation raise some ethical questions. First, some argue that paired donation and list donation involve the giving of organs for valuable consideration, which is forbidden by current law. By way of proof, consider one of the main arguments in support of paired and list donation. Supporters claim that these forms of donation would increase the organ supply by encouraging those who would not normally donate to give an organ. What encourages these donors, or perhaps entices them, is that once they give an organ their loved one will gain a corresponding advantage by receiving either transplanted organ or a higher place on the organ waiting list. Without this enticement, many of these donors would probably not even consider giving. Donation in these instances involves more than freely offering an organ with no expectation of gaining any advantage from the gift. Paired and list donation are, some might argue, forms of organ trading. They thus corrupt the morally preferable practice of pure gifting.

The second criticism applies only to list donation. As a quick reminder, list donation occurs when a donor gives a kidney to the transplant waiting list and the donor's intended recipient then in turn either receives the next available biologically compatible kidney or gains a higher place on the waiting list. Generally, those who are waiting for a blood-type O kidney face the longest wait of the different blood-types on the list because of the scarcity of O organs. An ethical dilemma arises when a person who is waiting for a blood-type O kidney has a biologically incompatible donor who is willing to donate a kidney to the general waitlist in return for seeing his or her loved one receive the next available O kidney or move up the O waitlist. Those who do not have a willing list donor must then wait even longer for a relatively scarce O kidney in an already slow moving line. By this argument, fairness requires prohibiting list donation, or at least list donations involving an intended recipient with O blood-type, even if permitting this practice means that more patients get organs because more organs are available.

The third criticism also applies only to list donation. As noted previously, with list donation, the intended recipient of a donor who gives a kidney to the general kidney list receives a deceased donor kidney. Deceased donor kidneys have a shorter average lifespan than living donor kidneys. The ethical dilemma raised in this criticism is whether or not it is just for an intended recipient to receive a kidney that will not last as long as the kidney that the intended recipient's donor is donating to the general kidney list.

The fourth criticism is of list donation's impact on paired donation. It is estimated that for a realistic maximum conversion rate using paired donation there must be around 250 incompatible pairs registered. With 250 pairs, roughly 50 percent of the recipients of these pairs would receive a kidney. To reach a 55 percent conversion rate, the registry would need 5,000 incompatible pairs. Currently, most paired donation registries are aiming at 250 pairs, but even this relatively modest number of pairs is difficult to generate. List donation only exacerbates this problem. When programs permit list donation, the number of incompatible pairs on the paired donation registry usually drops because these pairs are turning to list donation. When these pairs leave the paired donation registry, it becomes more difficult for paired donation programs to achieve the realistic maximum conversion rate.

Finally, some argue that paired donation and list donation will not substantially affect the supply of transplantable organs. Between the two of them, they have accounted for slightly more than 200 additional transplants over the six years they have been used. With nearly seventy thousand Americans waiting for kidneys, some see these options as welcome but wholly inadequate.

Periodical Bibliography

The following articles have been selected to supplement the diverse views presented in this chapter.

Jerry Adler	"Are Kidneys a Commodity?" *Newsweek*, May 26, 2008.
Jane E. Brody	"The Solvable Problem of Organ Shortages," *New York Times*, August 28, 2007.
Stephen J. Dubner and Steven D. Levitt	"Flesh Trade," *New York Times Magazine*, July 9, 2006.
The Economist	"Your Part or Mine?" November 18, 2006.
Josh Fischman	"Mix, Match, and Switch," *U.S. News & World Report*, October 16, 2006.
Amy L. Friedman	"Payment for Living Organ Donation Should Be Legalised," *British Medical Journal*, October 7, 2006.
Michele Goodwin	"The Organ Donor Taboo," *Forbes*, October 15, 2007.
Benjamin E. Hippen	"Organ Sales and Moral Travails," *CATO Policy Analysis*, March 20, 2008.
Kerry Howley	"Kidneys for Sale," *Reason*, June 2008.
Rupert Major	"Paying Kidney Donors: Time to Follow Iran?" *McGill Journal of Medicine*, vol. 11, no. 1, 2008.
Virginia Postrel	"Need Transplant Donors? Pay Them," *Los Angeles Times*, June 10, 2006.
Sally Satel	"Death's Waiting List," *New York Times*, May 15, 2008.

CHAPTER 3

What Are the Ethical Issues Surrounding Organ Donation?

Chapter Preface

Few things can be considered more devastating than the death of an infant, but some parents gain a measure of comfort despite their loss by donating their child's organs to another baby in need. However, during the summer of 2008, this procedure became controversial when an article published in the August 14 issue of the *New England Journal of Medicine* revealed that doctors at the Denver Children's Hospital had removed the hearts from three infants before they met the accepted standard of cardiac death. Critics of this procedure charge that the doctors committed infanticide.

The study, led by Dr. Mark Boucek, involved the removal of hearts from three infants who had severe brain damage; their parents had agreed to take them off life support. Under current medical rules, hearts can be removed from organ donors if irreversible cardiac death has occurred. The recommended time to wait before determining that the heart has stopped beating is five minutes, according to the Institute of Medicine (IOM). For the first case, the Denver team waited three minutes, less than the IOM recommends, but within the standard used by some doctors. However, the doctors took out the hearts of the second and third infants only 75 seconds after their hearts had stopped. The doctors contend they waited less time to increase the chances that the hearts would be viable. According to the *New England Journal of Medicine* article, all three recipients of the hearts in question were alive six months later, compared to fourteen of the seventeen infants who received heart transplants after the standard wait.

Situations such as this have created concern that transplant surgeons are blurring the line between life and death. Rob Stein, writing for *The Washington Post*, explains the controversy when he writes: "Critics, however, are questioning the propriety of removing hearts from patients, especially babies, who are not brain-dead. . . . Some even said the operations are tantamount to murder." John Smeaton, the director of the Society for the Protection of Unborn Children, the leading pro-life organization in Britain, is among those who share this view. He opines, "The essential line taken by the paper's authors is that it really doesn't matter whether the patient is dead or not." Despite these concerns, other transplant centers are likely to follow the Denver method, which could help save the lives of some of the fifty infants who require a heart transplant each year. The Denver Children's Hospital also intends to continue using the new procedure.

As this debate over infant donation shows, organ donation is a medically and ethically complex issue. The authors in this chapter evaluate some of these moral controversies.

> *"Since there will always be a shortage of suitable organs and tissues for transplant, the current system of obtaining organs and allotting them must be more carefully defined."*

A Variety of Ethical Issues Surround Organ Donation

Gerald D. Coleman

Gerald D. Coleman addresses several of the ethical issues surrounding organ donation in the following viewpoint. According to Coleman, these issues include receiving proper consent and avoiding conflict of interest between the doctors of the organ donor and the doctors who will perform the transplant operation. Coleman further asserts that several norms must be satisfied in order for an organ donation to be ethical, such as the age and health of the patient and the assurance that the removal of organs from the donor is for serious reasons. Coleman is the rector of Saint Patrick's Seminary in Menlo Park, California.

As you read, consider the following questions:

1. According to Coleman, how many people will require kidney transplants by 2010?

Gerald D. Coleman, *America*, vol. 196, March 5, 2007. Copyright © 2007. Republished with permission of America Press, conveyed through Copyright Clearance Center, Inc.

2. Why were Catholic moralists opposed to living organ transplantation prior to 1950, as explained by the author?

3. In the author's view, what are the two necessary motivating factors to justify organ transplantation?

The Organ Procurement and Transplant Network (OPTN) estimates that there are currently more than 89,000 potential organ candidates on waiting lists. In the past decade, the number of persons nationwide waiting for kidneys has more than doubled to at least 65,500 and could reach 100,000 by 2010. This growing number is being driven by older patients between 50 and 65 years old. Depending on geographic location, the average wait is from three to nine years.

The United Network for Organ Sharing (UNOS), which oversees transplantation for the federal government, calculates that every day 17 people die while waiting for a vital organ. Living kidney donations represent 94 percent of all living donations. Organ donation between living persons has now surpassed that of donations from deceased persons; adults account for 95 percent of transplants using kidneys from cadavers.

Allocating Organs Based on Age

Two recent cases highlight significant concerns.

While riding his Harley-Davidson motorcycle in 2002, 30-year-old Shawn Stringfellow drove off an interstate highway near Denver, Colo., and struck a construction barrel. The next day he was declared brain dead, while life support kept his heart beating. With his family's consent, calls went out to transplant centers that Stringfellow's two kidneys were available.

Clois Guthrie, an 85-year-old patient, was third on the regional organ waiting list for a kidney transplant. In light of his overall health condition, he likely had only a few more years to live. Two younger candidates were first and second on the list. One nephrologist on the transplant team argued that the kidneys could last decades if given to a younger patient. Another team member claimed that it is unethical to give a young kidney to an 85-year-old patient. Guthrie was then removed from the waiting list.

The allocation of a scarce resource is a moral issue. UNOS already has given patients younger than 18 an advantage by moving them to the front of the line for high-quality organs from donors younger than 35. In 2007 the U.S. Health Resources and Services Administration is expected to consider a national policy on the allocation of available organs for transplantation. [A report was issued in September 2007, but no mention was made of age restrictions.] While patients older than 79 would no longer be accepted, patients 70 to 79 would be considered for subpar organs from living donors, usually relatives.

The Ethics of Donations from Strangers

In another case, Herbert Davis, a 65-year-old physicist from Menlo Park, Calif., needed a new kidney. He had lived with damaged kidneys for decades as a result of a childhood infection. After four years of dialysis, he received his first kidney transplant in 1995. This transplanted kidney failed nine years later. His wife was not a compatible kidney match and sent an emotional letter to 140 friends and relatives pleading for a donation. One of them knew Matt Thompson.

Matt Thompson read the letter and felt that the plea was addressed to him. "I felt that God was compelling me to help out," he said. Thompson is a born-again Christian and has done missionary work in Brazil. He is married and has an infant daughter. Davis and Thompson had never met nor did they know each other. When Thompson contacted Davis's transplant program, he was turned down flat. He was not permitted to donate an organ to a stranger because of the medical risks involved. This is a regulation in many U.S. transplantation programs. Hospitals also worry that a donation from a stranger may involve undisclosed financial incentives.

Davis and Thompson then forged a friendship around the kidney transplant, however, and the situation changed. The hospital relented. "We started off as strangers, we moved to friends, and after the surgery, we're now a family," Thompson explained. The surgery successfully took place on November 14, 2006, at the University of California Medical Center, San Francisco.

In this case, the moral issue was rooted in medicine's "do no harm" principle that requires physicians to justify performing risky surgery on a healthy donor. Noted bioethicist Arthur Caplan has explained that principle: "The closer the relationship, the more medicine feels comfortable saying, 'We'll subject you to risk.'" He argues that there is a scientific consensus that "ethically, you don't force relationships."

Dr. John Scandling, medical director of the adult kidney and pancreas transplant program at Stanford University, stresses the risk involved: "It's major surgery. You can die." Stanford bioethicist David Magnus adds that the process whereby Herbert Davis attained the kidney donated by Matt Thompson is "inappropriate, absolutely." Says Magnus, "Living donor programs aren't intended to find ways for people to artificially become friends, but to allow people who are close friends to donate." He characterized the Davis-Thompson arrangement as "just a way of skirting the system." Stanford Medical Center restricts organ donations to friends and family.

At California Pacific Medical Center, surgeons evaluate "relationship" on a case-by-case basis using the criterion that "there is no sliding scale of friendship." It is critical to ensure that donors have the right motives and are not being coerced.

Donations Should Be Based on Fairness

Some argue that just as we have a right to donate to the political parties and charities of our choice, so should we be able to choose to whom to give our organs. In practice, however, this means that those who have the most compelling stories and the means to advertise their plight tend to be the ones who get the organs—rather than those most in need. This strikes some ethicists as unfair. Unlike monetary gifts, they argue, organ transplantation requires the involvement of social structures and institutions, such as transplantation teams and hospitals. Hence, the argument goes, these donations are legitimately subject to societal requirements of fairness, and transplantation centers should refuse to permit the allocation of organs on the basis of anything but morally relevant criteria.

Robert D. Truog,
"The Ethics of Organ Donation by Living Donors,"
New England Journal of Medicine, *August 4, 2005.*

At the University of California, Davis transplant program, strangers are allowed to donate but must do so anonymously for the patients most in need.

Four Ethical Issues Surround Organ Donation

These two cases raise significant ethical issues. Should the presumption for an organ transplant be that younger people are always to be preferred since organs are too often squandered on the old? And should donors be limited to family or close friends?

While organ or tissue transplantation from a dead to a living person presents no moral problem in itself, four other issues are relevant: the expense involved in the medical procedure, assurance of the total brain death of the donor, attaining proper consent and assuring the appropriate separation between the physicians who make the donation medically possible and those who belong to and participate in the transplantation team. This avoids a conflict of interest—for example, if a doctor were on the transplant team and at the same time were the patient's doctor, he/she could hasten death to make the organ more quickly available.

Before 1950, Catholic moralists argued that living organ transplantation was unethical because it necessarily involved harming and injuring a person's body. The principle of totality forbids mutilation. In 1956, Gerald Kelly, S.J., suggested a different way of viewing organ donations when he wrote that "by a sort of instinctive judgment . . . the giving of a part of one's body to help a sick man is not only morally justifiable, but, in some instances, actually heroic." He limited his moral reasoning justifying organ transplantation to "the principle of fraternal love or charity," provided that there was only limited harm to the donor.

Father Kelly and later Catholic moralists distinguished between anatomical integrity and functional integrity. Anatomical integrity refers to the physical integrity of the human body and functional integrity refers to its efficiency. If a person were missing a kidney, for example, there would be a lack of anatomical integrity, but there is functional integrity since one healthy kidney provides efficiency.

Papal Views on Organ Donation

These moral judgments for both living and deceased organ donations found their way into papal approval.

- In 1995, [Pope] John Paul II declared in his encyclical *The Gospel of Life* that our daily life "should be filled with self-giving love for others. A particularly praise-worthy example is the donation of organs, performed in an ethically acceptable manner, with a view to offering a chance of health and even of life itself to the sick who sometimes have no other hope."

- In an "Address to the International Congress of Transplantation," in 2000, the pope described the practice of organ donation as "a genuine act of love."

- The Catechism of the Catholic Church identifies organ donation as a concrete sign of solidarity with other members of the human community.

- The Ethical and Religious Directives for Catholic Health Care Services notes that "Catholic health care institutions should encourage and provide the means whereby those who wish to do so may arrange for the donation of their organs and bodily tissue."

Ethical Standards Must Be Met

In light of this Catholic tradition, the two cases summarized above suggest certain challenges and guidelines. Since there will always be a shortage of suitable organs and tissues for transplant, the current system of obtaining organs and allotting them must be more carefully defined. The overall health benefit to the candidate needs to be a significant factor in allotments.

Charity and human solidarity must be the motivating factors that justify organ transplantation. While the sale of organs by living donors is common practice in some countries, it is always unethical and should be made illegal. Human solidarity must be considered when evaluating the relationship between the candidate and the donor.

The Internet has vastly expanded opportunities to link donors with patients by way of e-mail pleas or urgent postings on craigslist.org or other sites (like www.matchingdonors.

com). Behind the sale of organs is the poverty of the individual willing to sell, not to mention the financial interest of any middlemen involved in transacting the sale. Organ transplantation for sale, however, is ethically wrong. In the United States, it is illegal to receive payment for a donated organ. A "free market" for the buying and selling of organs radically subverts the basic motives of charity and human solidarity.

Total brain death must be maintained as a criterion before organ transplantation is ethical. In the case of an anencephalic infant, for instance, it is not permissible to remove organs because the child's cerebral cortex has not developed. Yet the absence of the higher brain does not alone constitute death. At the same time, it is permissible to place an adult or infant on a respirator to ensure that blood will continue permeating the organs so that they could be suitable for transplant after clinical signs have certified that total brain death has occurred.

In sum, the following ethical norms should inform organ transplantations:

1. A patient's general health condition and age should be a consideration.

2. Unless the donation is anonymous, some level of authentic connection must be present between the donor and the patient.

3. Such a level of connection establishes a reason to justify proportionately the risk to the donor.

4. The functional integrity of a donor must never be impaired, even though the donor's anatomical integrity is compromised.

5. Stewardship of one's body demands that we have a serious reason for harming the health and anatomical integrity of our body.

6. Fraternal love must justify all organ transplantations. This principle negates any monetary gain. Selling one's organs is intrinsically reprehensible. "Cash for flesh" must never be tolerated.

7. The donor's consent must be fully informed and freely given.

| "*[Donation after cardiac death] can provide comfort and support to donor families.*"

Declaration of Cardiac Death Is an Ethical Reason for Organ Donation

J.L. Bernat, et al.

In the following viewpoint, J.L. Bernat and his co-authors contend that it is ethical to donate organs after a patient has experienced cardiac death, rather than requiring brain death to have occurred. According to Bernat, organ donations after cardiac death (DCD) save lives and do not violate the rules regarding donor death. Bernat and his co-authors further explain how organs retrieved after cardiac death can be best allocated. Bernat is a professor of neurology at Dartmouth Medical School.

As you read, consider the following questions:

1. How do Bernat and his co-authors define the dead donor rule?
2. What organ has been successfully transplanted after cardiac death, according to the authors?

J.L. Bernat, et al., "Report of a National Conference on Donation After Cardiac Death," *American Journal of Transplantation*, vol. 6, June 2006, pp. 281–282, 286–287. © 2006 The Authors. Reproduced by permission of Blackwell Publishers.

3. According to the authors, when should the final phase of informed consent occur?

A national conference on organ donation after cardiac death (DCD) was convened in Philadelphia on April 7 and 8, 2005, to address the increasing experience of DCD and to affirm the ethical propriety of transplanting organs from such donors. Participants represented the broad spectrum of the medical community, including neuroscientists, critical care professionals and distinguished bioethicists.

Determining Death by a Cardiopulmonary Criterion

A prospective organ donor's death may be determined by either cardiopulmonary (DCD) or neurologic criteria (donation after brain death [DBD]). The term *donation after cardiac death (DCD)* clearly indicates that death precedes donation. Death determination in the DCD patient mandates the use of a cardiopulmonary criterion to prove the absence of circulation. The cardiopulmonary criterion may be used when the donor does not fulfill brain death criteria. The ethical axiom of organ donation necessitates adherence to the dead donor rule: the retrieval of organs for transplantation should not cause the death of a donor.

In clinical situations that fulfill either brain death criteria or the circulatory criterion of death, the diagnosis of death requires the determination of both *cessation of functions* and *irreversibility.*

Cessation of functions is recognized by an appropriate clinical examination that reveals the absence of responsiveness, heart sounds, pulse and respiratory effort. In applying the circulatory criterion of death in non-DCD circumstances, clinical examination alone may be sufficient to determine cessation of circulatory and respiratory functions. However, the urgent time constraints of DCD may require more definitive proof of cessation of these functions by the use of confirmatory tests. Confirmatory tests (e.g. intra-arterial monitoring or Doppler study) should be performed in accordance with the hospital protocol to assure the family and the hospital professional staff that the patient is dead.

The 1997 Institute of Medicine (IOM) report suggested that "accepted medical detection standards include electrocardiographic changes consistent with absent heart function by electronic monitoring and zero pulse pressure as determined by monitoring through an arterial catheter." Conference participants concluded that electrocardiographic (ECG) silence is not required for the determination of death, because the criterion for determining death is the absence of circulation. However, if ECG silence is determined, it may be used as a confirmatory test for absent circulation because ECG silence is sufficient to show absence of circulation.

Irreversibility is recognized by persistent cessation of function during an appropriate period of observation. Based on a cardiopulmonary criterion, DCD donor death occurs when respiration and circulation have ceased and cardiopulmonary function *will not resume spontaneously.* This meaning of "irreversibility" also has been called the "permanent" cessation of respiration and circulation. If data show that autoresuscitation (spontaneous resumption of circulation) cannot occur and if there is no attempt at artificial resuscitation, it can be concluded that respiration and circulation have ceased permanently.

In clinical situations in which death is expected, once respiration and circulation cease (irrespective of electrical cardiac activity), the period of observation necessary to determine that circulation will not recur spontaneously (autoresuscitation) may be only a few minutes. Current data on autoresuscitation indicate that the relevant event is cessation of circulation, not cessation of electrical activity. When life-sustaining therapy is withdrawn, based on the limited data

available, spontaneous circulation does not return after 2 min-
[utes] of cessation of circulation.

Establishing the Length of Observation

An Organ Procurement Organization (OPO) survey conducted
for the DCD conference determined that 92 percent of all
OPOs use a 5-minute interval from asystole [no cardiac electrical activity] to the declaration of death, consistent with the
IOM recommendations. Nevertheless, three OPOs use an interval of 2 minutes and one OPO uses an interval of 4 minutes.

The Society of Critical Care Medicine (SCCM) concluded
that "at least 2 minutes of observation is required, and more
than 5 minutes is not recommended."

The IOM and SCCM recommendations were expert judgments. Subsequent studies have not been conducted to provide a statistically valid basis for determining the minimum
duration of observation for ruling out the possibility of autoresuscitation. Until additional data are available, the time in-
tervals used by physicians to observe the absence of circulation and thereby certify death may vary. Conference
participants supported the wording of the SCCM that for
DCD "at least 2 minutes of observation is required, and more
than 5 minutes is not recommended." When death is declared
following these considerations, no further time is required before recovery events may be initiated.

Appropriate agencies of the Department of Health and
Human Services should fund observational studies on the frequency of autoresuscitation in DCD patients and other patients dying after withdrawal of life-sustaining therapy. However, the cardiopulmonary criterion of death (irreversible
cessation of circulatory and respiratory function) applies to all
patients who lose circulation, regardless of organ donor
status. . . .

Allocation of DCD Organs for Transplantation

Strategies for DCD organ allocation were considered to provide equitable access for DCD organs while sustaining incentives for DCD recovery. The economic impact of DCD on a transplant center's interest in accepting DCD organs was also addressed, noting that the rate of DGF [delayed graft function] is almost doubled for DCD kidneys (40.1%), compared with non-DCD SCD [standard criteria donors] kidneys (21.2%). The yield of organs from DCD is clearly less than that for SCD, but slightly better than that achieved by ECD [expanded criteria donors].

Among kidney transplants from deceased donors who did not meet the ECD definition, overall adjusted 1- and 3-year allograft survivals were 90% and 80% for SCD and 89% and 80% for DCD recipients, respectively. Among transplants from donors who met the ECD definition, overall 1- and 3-year adjusted allograft survivals were 83% and 71% for ECD transplants and 81% and 70% for DCD/ECD kidneys, respectively.

The SRTR [Scientific Registry of Transplant Recipient] analysis of OPTN [Organ Procurement and Transplantation Network] outcome data provided important references for the working group's consideration of allocation. Given current donor and candidate acceptance criteria, allograft survival for similar subgroups (with or without ECD status, with or without DGF) of DCD and DBD kidneys were found to be comparable.

Allocating Kidneys

The OPOs are not required to include DCD kidneys in the "payback" process, in exchange for receipt of a zero-antigen mismatched kidney by a transplant center in the OPO's DSA. The DCD kidneys are allocated to zero-antigen mismatched patients locally, and then they are allocated by local, regional and national distribution. The allocation policy should hasten

The Effectiveness of DCD for Each Organ

Different organs tolerate different periods of reduced blood flow; therefore, technical challenges and success rates of DCD [donation after cardiac death] vary for different organs. For renal transplants, DCD organs currently provide comparable results to those from brain dead donors, and at times better results than from extended criteria donation (ECD) by brain dead donors. DCD liver transplants offer mixed results. . . .

DCD lung transplantation is a new and evolving practice. DCD heart transplant remains rare due to the heart's extreme sensitivity to ischemia, but some experts anticipate the development of this practice.

New York State Task Force on Life and the Law,
Donation After Cardiac Death, *April 17, 2007.*

the process (organ placement) by which OPOs obtain transplant center acceptance for a DCD organ. To counter the disincentive to recover DCD, the work group participants recommended that DCD not be used in calculating outcomes for OPTN or CMS [Centers for Medicare and Medicaid Services] reports of center performance.

With current data showing equivalency in graft and patient survivals of DCD and DBD primary kidney transplants despite higher DGF rates in DCD organs, conference participants were reluctant to recommend changes in the current DCD allocation policy.

If there is no local center available to recover DCD organs, the OPTN computer match run should be followed regionally. The accepting regional program must be willing to procure to receive the DCD organs. For DCD kidney-only donors, the regional center could recover and retain one kidney for its patient. The other kidney is offered locally to a willing center. If there is no accepting local center, then the second kidney will be offered through the UNOS Organ Center according to the OPTN computer match program. . . .

Allocating Livers and Pancreases

Participants recommended that the OPTN require centers to list candidates who are willing to accept DCD liver offers. Given the higher risk of graft failure for DCD livers compared with SCD livers candidates should be counseled regarding the risk of DCD organ acceptance, with informed consent obtained at the time of listing. The effect of DCD on outcomes may influence recipient selection. The hazard ratio of death following transplantation exceeds the risk of death while waiting on the list for candidates at certain MELD [Model for End-Stage Liver Disease] scores.

The work group participants recommended that DCD donor liver placement follow the current allocation algorithm, with distribution stratified by local recovery and allocation followed by regional offers. Parallel (backup) offers should be made to expedite placement.

Successful pancreas transplantation has been reported from DCD at the University of Wisconsin. The work group participants recommended that the current OPTN pancreas allocation algorithm be followed, with local DSA priority given to combined kidney/pancreas candidates or pancreas-alone candidates who have been listed as willing to accept a DCD pancreas.

The work group participants considered the information that should be shared with a potential transplant recipient of a DCD organ to achieve informed consent. This aspect of the deliberations was controversial. Some of the participants recommended full disclosure of the donor circumstances of death, because the outcome, especially for DCD liver allograft recipients, might be less than that achieved by transplantation of DBD organs.

The process of informed consent should be done in phases, with the current characteristics of the deceased donor pool discussed at the outset of a patient listing. This initial consent discussion should include the transplantation of organs from donors with varying degrees of risk of failure compared with an ideal donor. Final consent should be obtained at the time of the proposed transplantation, when the physicians have a more precise assessment of the risks associated with undergoing a DCD (or ECD) transplant versus the risk of waiting for the next available donor (considering the candidate's severity of disease and mortality risk at the time of the offer).

The Media, Public Perceptions and DCD

The work group participants were asked to assemble comprehensive information for different audiences—the transplant community, other professional disciplines and the press and the general public—and disseminate this conference report in an informative but not promotional manner. The expansion of policies related to DCD reflects advances in the practice of medicine. Families who want their loved ones to be an organ and tissue donor should no longer be excluded from the opportunity of donation nor should they have to bear the responsibility of raising the DCD option to the medical care team.

The public message to be conveyed about DCD is listed below:

- DCD honors donor wishes in the continuum of quality end-of-life care.

- DCD can provide comfort and support to donor families.

- DCD saves lives.

The National Conference on DCD affirmed DCD as an ethically acceptable practice of end-of-life care, capable of increasing the number of deceased-donor organs available for successful transplantation.

> *"[Donation after cardiac death] proto-*
> *cols remove organs from a donor who*
> *is not irreversibly dead; if the whole*
> *brain is not yet dead, the patient can-*
> *not be dead."*

Declaration of Cardiac Death Is Not an Adequate Reason for Organ Donations

Leslie Whetstine, et al.

Cardiac death is not a legitimate justification for organ dona-
tion, Leslie Whetstine contends in the following viewpoint. Whet-
stine asserts that donation after cardiac death (DCD) is not
ethical because death can only occur if the brain has died. Fur-
thermore, the author argues, DCD is dependent on an inaccu-
rate understanding of resuscitation and could lead to organ re-
moval occurring before the patient is brain dead. Whetstine is a
professor of philosophy at Walsh University in North Canton,
Ohio.

As you read, consider the following questions:

1. In the author's view, what is the first shortcoming of the Uniform Determination of Death Act?

Leslie Whetstine, et al., "Pro/Con Ethics Debate: When Is Dead Really Dead?" *Critical Care*, vol. 9, December 2005, pp. 538–539. © 2005 BioMed Central Ltd. Reproduced by permission.

2. Why does Whetstine argue that the inability to auto-resuscitate should not be used to determine when death has occurred?

3. What is the dead donor rule, as defined by the author?

The scenario: A 45-year-old female patient arrives in the emergency department after having complained of a headache and progresses to unresponsiveness. She is placed on mechanical ventilation and a CAT scan of her brain shows massive intracranial bleed. The family is assured she will probably progress to brain death but she doesn't. After two days in the intensive care unit, she continues with gasping ventilations and some flexion to pain in one arm. All other brain functions are absent. Her hemodynamics and other organ function are stable. The family desires the patient to be an organ donor but she is clearly not brain dead. It is suggested to the family that the patient can still donate under the 'Donation after Cardiac Death' (DCD) rules. Life support can be withdrawn and she can be pronounced dead using asystole [a form of cardiac arrest in which the heart stops beating and there is no electrical activity in the heart] as a criterion rather than brain death, following which organs can be taken for transplantation after a variable period of time to rule out 'auto-resuscitation'. Would you recommend this procedure?

The question that arises from this case is: Is the DCD donor truly dead at the moment of organ recovery? The answer depends on two things: first, on what concept of death we are using; and second, what version of irreversibility we find most compelling. It is beyond the scope of this analysis to examine the appropriate conceptual definition of death, but suffice to say that the traditional concept of death is the irreversible cessation of the integrated functioning of the organism as a whole. I will argue that DCD does not fulfill this definition.

One Way to Declare Death

The Uniform Determination of Death Act (UDDA) established that death could be declared by either the irreversible cessation of circulatory functions or the irreversible cessation of the entire brain, including the brain stem. DCD advocates cite this statute as evidence that DCD is a legitimate practice using the circulatory criterion. The UDDA may appear to support DCD but only if we construe a bifurcated rather than a unitary definition of death that does not require the permanent cessation of the organism as a whole but only of certain parts of it. The UDDA claimed it did not suggest two different types of death but that either of the two criteria were necessary and sufficient conditions for death. We cannot embark on a critical analysis of this legislation here but it has three primary shortcomings: First, it failed to define the critical term 'irreversible'; second, irreversible absence of circulation is sufficient for death but not necessary; and third, irreversible absence of circulation may be a mechanism of death, but it is not death itself, which has always been regarded as brain death. As quoted from the *New England Journal of Medicine*, "It is clear that a person is not dead until his brain is dead. The time honoured criteria of the stoppage of the heart beat and circulation are indicative of death only when they persist long enough for the brain to die."

Advocates of DCD take a soft-line interpretation of irreversibility. They argue that if resuscitation has been proscribed and if the person cannot spontaneously resuscitate (auto-resuscitation), the person is irreversibly dead as a practical matter. But a moral decision to not restore function does not ensure the clinical state of death has been fulfilled. Moreover, inability to auto-resuscitate cannot be used to determine when death has occurred as many people who cannot auto-resuscitate can be resuscitated with an intervention. Finally, the time period in which auto-resuscitation may occur has not been sufficiently studied to make a determination that

Patients Whose Hearts Have Stopped Can Recover

It is now widely known that a patient whose heart has stopped beating for 15 minutes after a heart attack can recover if they are treated by cooling the body to 33 degrees Celsius, cardio-pulmonary by-pass, cardioplegia, that is, stopping the heart beat chemically, and a slow increase in oxygenation for 24 hours. Up to 80 percent of these patients can be discharged from hospital, 55 percent having a good neurological outcome. Clearly, the assumption made by physicians that a patient is dead five minutes after the heart has stopped beating is incorrect.

John B. Shea, "Organ Donation: The Inconvenient Truth,"
Catholic Insight, *September 2007.*

two or five minutes of asystole will preclude it. The fact that a person proscribes resuscitation or cannot auto-resuscitate does not make one dead at that precise moment, but prognosticates death and suggests one has entered a dying process that may ultimately lead to irreversible death.

Organ donation operates under the dead donor rule (DDR), which stipulates that organs may not be removed prior to death nor may organ procurement cause or hasten death. DCD fails to satisfy the DDR on three counts: First, it manipulates the definition of irreversibility based on a moral position not to resuscitate; second, it appeals to fallacious logic that because one cannot auto-resuscitate then one is dead; and third, it focuses solely on the circulatory criterion endorsed by the UDDA, which does not immediately correlate with brain status. Generally speaking, using the circulatory criterion would not be problematic as its absence will inevitably cause total brain failure. In DCD, however, the need for speed becomes a factor such that organs will be removed before the requisite time it takes for the brain to die as cessation of cardio-respiratory functions does not cause the brain to die immediately.

Brain Death Determines Death

If the body can be resuscitated, we have to question if it was ever really dead given our conventional notion of death as a finality from which one cannot be returned or resurrected from under any circumstances. DCD protocols remove organs from a donor who is not irreversibly dead; if the whole brain is not yet dead, the patient cannot be dead.

> *"A sweeping ban on the involvement of prisoners as organ donors unjustifiably deprives them of a unique opportunity to engage in productive acts."*

Prisoners Should Be Permitted to Donate Organs

L.D. de Castro

In the following viewpoint, L.D. de Castro asserts that prisoners should have the right to donate their kidneys in exchange for a stay of execution or a commuted sentence. He argues that the vulnerable situation of prisoners is not a valid reason to prevent them from making the decision to donate, since prisoners have often shown the ability to contribute to society. According to de Castro, a policy of organ donations from prisoners, if equipped with safeguards, would benefit the prisoners and organ recipients. L.D. de Castro is a professor of philosophy at the University of the Philippines.

As you read, consider the following questions:

1. In de Castro's view, from what must prisoners be protected?

L.D. de Castro, "Human Organs from Prisoners: Kidneys for Life," *Journal of Medical Ethics*, vol. 29, June 2003, pp. 171–175. Copyright © 2003 British Medical Association. Reproduced by permission of BMJ Publishing Group Ltd, conveyed through Copyright Clearance Center.

2. According to de Castro, how do prisoners benefit from organ donation?

3. In the view of the author, why should the family of the proposed donor be consulted?

Kidneys for life is the name that has been given to a proposal in the Philippines to allow prisoners to save their lives or to have their prison sentences commuted by donating kidneys for transplantation. The catchy phrase has been used to refer to convicts who might wish to take advantage of the opportunity whether they are on death row or not. The slogan takes on a peculiar meaning because the donors are invited to save their own lives and not necessarily those of the transplant recipients. From this standpoint, the preservation of the recipients' lives is only a side effect that the donors might not even care about. There are, however, good reasons for allowing organ donations by prisoners. Under certain conditions, such donations can be very beneficial not only to the recipients but to the prisoners themselves.

Admittedly, prisoners are in a very vulnerable position. They require protection from coercion and exploitation. Paternalism can however, be overdone. Overprotection can work against the vulnerable people that it aims to protect. The prohibition on the involvement of prisoners in organ transplantation is a type of overprotection that can be exploitative. This kind of exploitation can have worse consequences for the prisoner than underprotection. The vulnerability of prisoners does not, in itself, make it wrong for them to be involved as organ donors.

Notwithstanding the restrictive character of their environment, prisoners can make genuinely independent decisions. When it can be reasonably ascertained that their decisions are truly their own, society should recognize an obligation to help them implement such decisions. This is particularly important when prisoners make the decision to donate an organ as a way of asserting their religious faith and performing a sacrifice in atonement for their sins. . . .

Prisoners Can Make Informed Decisions

The reasons that have been given for opposing the involvement of prisoners in organ transplants do not indicate that such involvement is necessarily or inherently wrong. One view that comes close to being a claim that prisoner involvement is inherently wrong holds that prisoners, by virtue of their being imprisoned, are necessarily trapped in a coercive environment. It appears to be taken for granted in ethical discourse that incarcerated individuals are not in a position to make free and informed decisions. The conditions of imprisonment are themselves coercive and not conducive to free decision making. Prisoners are liable to exploitation and manipulation because their control of their lives is considerably restricted. Their day to day options are severely limited and this condition is inherent in imprisonment.

Still, these limitations do not necessarily prevent prisoners from making a free and informed decision regarding the possibility of making an organ donation. While there are many prisoners who are confined under severely inhibiting conditions, there are those who have been given relatively lighter sentences and live under more open terms of confinement. There are many facilities designed to involve prisoners in productive activities. There are correctional centres where convicts are engaged in farming, handicraft, and other livelihood projects from which they are permitted to earn money. At these centres, prisoners live productive lives and gain empowerment in the process. Some criminals have been helped to a life of prayer and even of ministry that provides a context for their possible involvement as organ donors.

A number of high profile criminals have been held up to the public as examples of convicted prisoners who have transcended the conditions of their incarceration. They have overcome the vulnerabilities associated with prison life. Many of them have also made valuable contributions to society. They may not constitute the majority but there are enough of them who might consider making a gift of a transplantable organ to a person in need.

Even if the conditions of imprisonment are usually coercive in nature, there are prisoners who are capable of transcending these conditions and acting as autonomous agents. They can be in command of their decisions. These prisoners can be responsible enough to take risks for themselves and to make genuine sacrifices for the rest of society.

Banning Prisoner Donation Is Unethical

Although prisoners require protection because of their vulnerable situation, the nature of the protection provided has to be calibrated to fit their specific vulnerabilities. A blanket prohibition against their involvement as organ donors may be useful on the basis of a general presumption that the conditions of imprisonment are coercive to the point that free decision making is rendered impossible. If, however, it is possible to attain a reasonable level of confidence in a given situation that a particular prisoner can understand the options available and decide freely, a comprehensive ban on organ donation will serve more as an unjustified restriction rather than as a welcome protection.

Vulnerabilities should not be regarded as permanently disabling conditions. They are weaknesses that can be overcome and they should be viewed as difficulties to be overcome. An area of vulnerability need not, in itself, disqualify a person from becoming an organ donor. Instead, it should signal the necessity of providing assistance to ascertain that a person is genuinely motivated and, if so, is in a position to achieve a noble purpose by participating in a freely chosen course of action.

A sweeping ban on the involvement of prisoners as organ donors unjustifiably deprives them of a unique opportunity to engage in productive acts that stand to be beneficial not only to renal patients but to themselves. Prisoners ought to be regarded differently from ordinary persons only in so far as they are being punished in accordance with the law. Restrictions on their actions are justifiable only to the extent that these restrictions follow from the terms of their confinement based on applicable judicial orders. Other than those that are mandated by pertinent courts, any restrictions must be regarded as excessive and unjust.

When a prisoner expresses an unequivocal desire to donate an organ, a prohibition has to be justified more strongly than by a general presumption that coercive conditions prevail whenever prisoners make decisions. A paternalistic stance has to be weighed in relation to the loss of possible benefits and the likely burden to those involved.

If the possible benefits from the involvement of prisoners as organ donors are so great (human lives saved or enhanced) and the risk of serious harm is small, an absolute prohibition on the practice would itself be unethical for another reason—by prohibiting the practice, we could be taking away benefits not only from organ recipients but from the donors themselves. That benefit consists of the prisoners' opportunity to make an organ donation as a means of reparation for their "sins". . . .

Prisoners Must Be Protected from Abuse

Rather than completely prohibiting prisoners' involvement in organ transplantation, the proper course of action is to put safety nets in place to ensure that their particular vulnerabilities cannot be exploited.

Like any other activity that can bring unexpected but coveted relief from a difficult situation, kidneys for life is open to abuse. Any legitimate activity is liable to exploitation through creative but wicked moneymaking schemes, especially if it is characterised by the prospect of a windfall type outcome. There is a possibility of collusion between prisoners eager to save their lives and prison officials who might see in the procedure a creative opportunity to make money. Especially in an economically impoverished environment, kidneys for life and organs for money can easily form a convenient merger.

This possibility has to be anticipated and avoided. Safeguards . . . have to be put in place. One should not, however, be afraid to pursue a novel initiative just because it is liable to abuse.

Moreover, experience has taught us that the refusal of government to take controversial practices head on because of the fear that acknowledgement of the activity can be interpreted as giving official blessings has more often led to greater abuse and more problems. The existing organs for money black market is an example of an undesirable outcome of a general policy of non-involvement in anything that could be controversial.

This is not to deny the risk of abuse entirely. Measures to counter possible abuse can only be effective if the possibility is honestly recognized and anticipated in a guarded and timely fashion. . . .

How to Safeguard Prisoner Donations

A successful kidneys for life proposal should, of course, be equipped with safeguards to ensure that the objectives are not going to be defeated by the actual practice. One can think of the following measures that might be useful:

1. Legal representation: a prisoner is vulnerable in a number of respects. Professional representation ought to be provided to prevent these vulnerabilities from being exploited. A lawyer will be needed to look after the interests of prisoner/donors since the grounds for detention obviously have their roots in the law. Any procedure

Donations Will Improve Prisoners' Morals

What is gained by [organ] donation? (1) The saving of someone's life; (2) Relieving overcrowding in prisons; and (3) Redeeming the criminal. Would this not slow down recidivism, prodding inmates to rethink their future actions and lives? To save a person's life and thereby to spare a father's agony and a mother's grief is an act of humanity. This is an ethical and moral action, even if a reward is proffered. To let people die when there is a possible avenue of relief is not ethical or moral: why not ask the would-be recipient?

Clifford Earle Bartz,
"The Donation Inmate Organ Network (DION):
Giving Inmates Time Off for Organ Donation,"
Medicine and Health Rhode Island, *December 2005.*

that seeks to cancel some of the effects of that law in order to provide relief to a convict will require knowledge of legal nuances such as only a professional lawyer can provide.

2. The usefulness of psychological counselling also appears obvious in view of the type of pressures that bear on the prisoner and the prisoner's family when the kidneys for life option arises.

3. Consultation with the applicant's family. Family consultation can facilitate a broader base for evaluating the prisoner's options by situating it within the context of the kinship system that would have been partly responsible for early identity formation. The kinship system is also a support mechanism that enables an individual to make stable decisions in the face of external threats.

4. Determination that the detention facilities available to a particular prisoner/applicant are conducive to an acceptable level of independence in decision making. This is necessary in as much as there is a wide variation in the quality of detention facilities that provide a physical context for the decision making of prisoner/applicants. There has to be an independent examination by experts who can assess the conditions of detention and the effects that these may have on the prisoner's independence.

5. Independent committee review. Like any ethically contentious activity, the implementation of kidneys for life in particular instances can profit from an independent committee review conducted by members who have no personal stake in the prospective donation.

6. Sufficient waiting time before a prisoner's application is approved and implemented to ensure, among other things, that the intention is more than fleeting.

Prisoner Donors Should Be Compensated

It may be argued that if the main justification for a kidneys for life programme were the need to allow prisoners to manifest their repentance in consonance with religious beliefs, they should not have to be given rewards. Thus, they should not have to be entitled to a sentence commutation.

This objection appears to be valid and a decision to permit the involvement of prisoners as organ donors should not be premised on their being entitled to rewards. Nevertheless, the fact that the donor is a prisoner should not diminish society's appreciation for the value of the donation. A human organ is a priceless contribution regardless of whose body it comes from. Perhaps it should even be more greatly valued for being an organ coming from a person in a vulnerable situation.

If only for this reason, a prisoner/donor ought to be given just compensation for giving an organ. The reasons for giving a reward are not necessarily based on the donor's being a prisoner—any donor deserves just compensation. The form that a particular reward takes may, however, be adapted to the particular recipient's situation.

In general, the contribution is so valuable that it would be exploitative to accept it without just compensation. The fact that a person has been convicted of a crime should not give the rest of society the right to take advantage of his imprisonment.

A comprehensive ban on the involvement of prisoners as organ donors appears to be anchored in a need to protect the possible donors from harm. There are, however, situations when the donation of organs by prisoners can be very beneficial to the prisoners themselves.

Although prisoners require protection from coercion and exploitation, we have to remember that overprotection can also work against them. In the case of the kidneys for life proposal, overprotection can have worse consequences for the prisoner than underprotection. When it can be reasonably ascertained that their decisions are freely made, society should be ready to assist prisoners in implementing such decisions.

| "Would care be further compromised if prisoners refused to participate in donating an organ?"

Allowing Prisoners to Donate Organs Is Unethical

Jay Baruch

In the following viewpoint, Jay Baruch argues that prisoners should not be allowed to donate kidneys in exchange for reduced sentences. In Baruch's opinion, the vulnerability of prisoners means that they cannot give informed consent. In addition, he asserts that establishing prisoner organ programs could result in the exploitation of prisoners. Baruch is a professor of emergency medicine at Brown Medical School and the director of medical education for emergency medicine at Memorial Hospital of Rhode Island.

As you read, consider the following questions:

1. What did the National Transplant Act of 1984 prohibit, as explained by Baruch?

2. According to the author, what diseases were prisoners exposed to deliberately between the 1940s and 1970s?

Jay Baruch, "Prisoners and Organ Donation," *Medicine and Health Rhode Island*, vol. 88, December 2005, pp. 437–438. Reproduced by permission of Rhode Island Department of Health.

3. According to Baruch, what type of financial incentive does Wisconsin provide to organ donors?

The numbers are daunting. Over 79,000 patients in the United States await organ transplants; nearly 3,000 new patients are added to the waiting list each month. Few people would argue that the current system of altruistic organ donation isn't meeting the demand.

There are over 2 million prisoners in US [United States] jails and prisons. Mining that community as potential donors might appear to be a goldmine. And there might be added incentive if prisoners are compensated with reduced sentences.

Such a plan sounds attractive but for two questions. 1) Are there ethical reasons why we might not want to consider prisoners as potential donors? 2) Should donors ever be compensated for their organs—turning a donor into a vendor? Sixteen to seventeen people die each day waiting for a vital organ. While we focus on procurement, we shouldn't lose sight of where and who the organs come from, and how they're procured.

Economic and Physical Effects on Donors

The National Transplant Act of 1984 prohibited the use of organs to be "bought, sold, swapped or traded for any kinds of monetary gains." What is objectionable to the use of prisoner donors? Isn't the moral high road pocked with holes and contradictions? After all, prostitution is illegal but tolerated in the United States, where the body is exchanged for money. People are paid for donating plasma, sperm and ova, so why should we consider kidneys differently? Plasma, sperm and ova replenish themselves, and can be obtained by minimally invasive means. Donating a solid organ is a riskier venture, including severe pain, potential complications, the permanent absence of a body part and potential long-term medical and psychological sequelae [an aftereffect of injury]. These factors may be relevant when individuals contemplate donating ova or a kidney, but should they, unto themselves, determine policy?

These questions might seem trivial to people who will die without an organ transplant, offensive to people who consider body parts their personal property which should be marketable if desired, and unnecessary to people who point to the laws that prohibit such activity. But a vast illicit black market exists. Supporters of market-exchange for organs claim it's a win-win situation. Recipients who can afford the cost fly to countries with more lenient, or no, regulations on organ procurement and transplantation. And the vendors, largely from impoverished populations, are given a boost out of poverty. In respect to kidneys, the path is usually, "from poorer to more affluent bodies, from black and brown bodies to white ones, and from females to males." Most of the time, relief is temporary, and vendors slide back into debt.

Post-operative sequelae, moreover, such as pain, fatigue, and depression, may compromise the donors' ability to do the manual work they did before. Their poverty might hinder their ability to receive post-operative care. In the end, their situation may become more dire than before the surgery. Such an outcome runs counter to a basic tenet of medical practice in the United States, which is to do no harm. Even with altruistic donations, a generally healthy person accepts some degree of risk for a procedure that will benefit someone else. But the person has given consent, and accepted those risks.

What about those individuals who sell their organs? It can be argued that they gave their consent by entering the market in the first place. But at least by normative standards in the United States, their decision might not have been a genuinely informed one. They might have been uneducated, and unable to understand the risks. Their economic circumstances might have restricted their options. Saddled with debt, struggling to provide basic needs like food and clothing, they may have had little choice except to sell an organ.

Prisoners May Not Be Able to Give Consent

This argument raises the question of whether institutionalized persons can truly give informed consent. Their dependency on others, the pressure to conform, and fear of the consequences when they make decisions contrary to what is expected, exert pressure on the decision-making process. The Nuremburg Code of 1947, drafted as a response to the inhumane medical experiments conducted by the Nazis, opens with the following. "[The] person involved should have legal capacity to give consent, should be so situated as to be able to exercise free power of choice, without the intervention of any element of force, fraud, deceit, duress, over-reaching or other ulterior form of constraint or coercion."

Despite this code, there have been infamous clinical trials involving abuses of prisoners and other institutionalized persons. In 1972, the pharmaceutical industry was doing more than 90 percent of its experimental testing on prisoners. From the 1940s to the 1970s, incarcerated prisoners were deliberately infected with or exposed to malaria, typhoid fever, cancer cells, cholera in attempts to cure these diseases.

Many criticisms of these studies focus on whether the prisoners willingly gave their informed consent. There were concerns that prisoners were influenced to participate in clinical trials by offers of special privileges, or reduced sentences, or access to better medical care. To consent to treatment, patients must demonstrate decision-making capacity. This element can be problematic amid worries that prisons are replacing hospitals for the mentally ill.

Prisoners are vulnerable. Having lost their liberty, they depend on the penal system for food, clothing, safety and healthcare. (Prisoners are the only Americans who have a constitutional right to healthcare). Despite such a claim on the penal system, there have been reports of serious substandard medical care. Would care be further compromised if prisoners re-

A Prisoner Organ Donation Policy May Affect Jurors

Were prisoners allowed to trade a kidney to mitigate a death sentence, it may affect the actual imposition of the death penalty. With greater publicity surrounding these types of proposals/laws, potential jurors could be influenced and ultimately impose the death penalty more often with a potential societal benefit in mind. Jurors might hope that the convicted persons would choose to trade their kidney for their life. This would present a gross inequity for those unable or unwilling to donate a kidney and who might otherwise have not received a death sentence.

United Network for Organ Sharing Ethics Committee, "Ethics of Organ Donation from Condemned Prisoners," 2008. www.optn.org.

fused to participate in donating an organ, or, would donors be given special privileges that would entice others to do something they wouldn't ordinarily do?

The notion of payment or compensation is part of a heated and perplexing debate. Though direct payments are illegal in the US, states are developing and/or implementing other incentives. Wisconsin allows "tax deductions up to $10,000 for expenses such as travel, hotel bills, and lost wages when donating an organ." Similar bills were introduced in other states. Some argue that a treacherous line is being walked. How do you encourage donations without violating the law and making the inducements so attractive that people feel they must find a way to donate an organ? And, just as in clinical trials, the participant-donor undertakes a risk that may, or may not, directly benefit him/her.

Using Prisoners as Donors Will Corrupt Society

Mr. Bartz's provocative article raises these issues. [This viewpoint responds to an article written by Clifford Earle Bartz in the same issue.] Would prisoners be giving a truly informed and uncoerced consent? Would their extreme circumstances make them do something they wouldn't otherwise do if they were on the outside? Would some prisoners who are a match to a waiting organ recipient, perhaps the governor's son, be coerced into giving an organ? The experience from other countries with organ vendors, and some ethically murky experiences with prisoners in clinical trials in the United States, should serve as a warning. The use of institutionalized or impoverished populations for organs, even if they "consented" to the procedure, is ripe for abuse, especially in an environment where transparency may be difficult to monitor.

Some will argue that prisoners should not be discounted from donating organs solely because they lack liberty. Confinement in institutions doesn't necessarily deprive individuals of their right to consent or refuse medical care. Why should they be denied the opportunity to give the gift of life? I agree to an extent. If prisoners truly made an informed decision, and they would have come to the same decision if they weren't in prison, their status as prisoners might be morally irrelevant. However, if prisoners are offered a reduced sentence in exchange for an organ, the fact that s/he is in prison becomes relevant to the decision.

What would it say about us as a society if we permitted prisoners to offer up an organ? Could regulations be implemented and enforced? Could prisoners be protected from exploitation? Much has been written about practices in China, where the organs of executed prisoners—who may, or may not, have been dead—are sold on the open market. Could we convince the public in the United States and abroad that similar abuses weren't taking place here?

I concur with Mr. Bartz's passionate belief that we need to think more creatively to increase the supply of organs in this country. I admire the work that he has put into the project, and read with fascination the article in this issue as well as a previous article he had written on the Donation Inmate Organ Network. Body parts, I believe, fall outside the marketplace. An organ is priceless, and payment for any organ would be so incommensurate to its worth to the recipient that it would somehow cheapen it.

I acknowledge that using prisoners as donors, and offering compensation for organs, might save some lives. But I believe such a practice would corrupt us as a society. I have concerns about the exploitation of vulnerable populations. I worry that it could fortify preexisting barriers that impede people's willingness to donate, and in the end, further compromise the procurement process.

As it stands, the reliance on altruism and "the gift of life" hasn't generated the necessary number of organs. There are many reasons given for this shortfall: the role of physicians and nurses, public distrust, and the potential exploitation of populations already marginalized by the healthcare system. But as Mr. Bartz says, people are dying everyday in need of an organ. They'd take an organ from Dracula if it was available. That urgency shouldn't be forgotten, but we need to take cautious steps, being ever mindful of the tenet, "Do no harm."

> *"Children . . . are not viable replace-*
> *ments for an incompetent, ineffective,*
> *organ procurement system."*

Children Should Not Be Organ Donors

Michele Goodwin

In the following viewpoint, Michele Goodwin argues that minor siblings, particularly those under the age of thirteen, should not be used as live organ donors. Goodwin criticizes the practice of parents conceiving a child in the hopes that he or she will be a match for an ailing sibling. According to Goodwin, these so-called "designer babies" and the siblings who receive the transplant suffer psychologically and therefore these types of donations should be limited as much as possible. Goodwin is a professor of law at the University of Minnesota.

As you read, consider the following questions:

1. As stated by Goodwin, what was the chance that Marissa Ayala was a match for her sister?

2. According to a study cited by Goodwin, what percentage of sibling bone marrow donors experience posttraumatic stress disorder after donating?

Michele Goodwin, *Black Markets: The Supply and Demand of Body Parts*. New York: Cambridge University Press, 2006. Copyright © Cambridge University Press 2006. Reprinted with the permission of Cambridge University Press.

3. In the view of the author, what do children under the age of thirteen lack the capacity to do?

Headlines refer to them as "designer babies" and modern-day "angels." They are the children of *reproductive altruism*, specially conceived to save dying siblings. Some are born with the help of genetic manipulation, as was Adam Nash, a test tube baby, specially tested to have the exact cell type necessary for bone marrow transplantation to his sister who was diagnosed with Fanconi anemia. The Nashes are thought to be America's first couple to screen their embryos before implanting in the mother's womb for the purpose of harvesting bone marrow. However, 12 years before, Abe Ayala surgically reversed his vasectomy, hoping that his wife would become pregnant with a child who would save their daughter's life. They were unabashed about "making" Marissa to save Anissa. According to doctors at the time, the Ayalas had a 25 percent chance that Marissa would be a match for her teenage sister. One reporter noted, they "won that gamble too." Marissa Ayala was 14 months old when she underwent bone marrow harvesting for transplantation to her sister, Anissa, who was 17 years old.

The couples were very different; one Hispanic and the other white, hailing from different regions in the United States. The Nash family lived in Colorado and the Ayalas in California. The couples, however, were motivated by similar desires. Both were unwilling to accept the inevitable deaths of their daughters. The Nash family followed the development of pre-implantation genetic diagnosis; a process involving the removal of a single cell from embryos created through standard in vitro fertilization techniques and developed in a laboratory petri dish. Before implantation in the uterus, the embryos were tested for Fanconi and those exhibiting no signs of the disease were implanted.

It was not love for their daughters that troubled ethicists, but rather the shared passion to create children strictly for the purpose of aiding siblings. The psychological ramifications were unpredictable and continue to be; the Nashes eliminated the need for luck by employing science, but how will Adam adjust to the purpose of his birth? The Ayalas gambled on luck, but it seems possible that disappointment might have resulted from a mismatch.

The Ethics of Parenting

As a society, we do not police parent motivations for having children. Whether we should do so is not a new question, but seemingly settled by the Supreme Court's analysis on the right to parent. Years ago the country entered a slippery slope deciding that certain people were not "fit" for reproduction. Carrie Buck was one among thousands subjected to draconian procedures to ensure American society would not be overrun with those deemed less socially and culturally desirable. The pendulum has swung, although pressures continue to exist to constrain the birthing of some mothers, as so eloquently addressed by Professor Dorothy Roberts' scholarship. Today, heterosexual and homosexual couples can choose when and how to have children through a variety of means, including surrogacy, in vitro technology, or sperm and ova donation. The distinction, however, between the desire to parent and the aspiration to bear a child to save another is a matter of intent. Certainly less noble causes have inspired copulation and child making, whether to grow the family business, save a marriage, express ego, stimulate financial resources, or even the sublime romantic, sentimental reasons. Should parents espousing reproductive altruism be held to a different ethical standard than those with hidden, nonaltruistic motivations?

The births of Adam and Marissa raise serious doubts about the confluence of the rule of law, biotechnology, ethics, and parenting. Although an effort to ban "transplantation" parenting in England was recently overturned, U.S. legislators and courts have yet to address the issue of reproductive altruism, the practice of having children to save the lives of other children. Although selling children is illegal, U.S. law does not set limits on who can parent, nor on how many children couples may produce, or when or under what circumstances they may reproduce. Save for child sexual abuse, resulting in pregnancies and preterm illegal drug use, the right to parent is closely guarded and protected.

Producing an additional child to supply an organ or bone marrow for a living offspring is certainly not an easy decision to come by. The predecision considerations may be endless; economic concerns, social adjustment, and even fertility doubts may be part of the decision-making process. Can the family afford to raise another child? The potential for disharmony and anger between the children rather than romantic notions of unconditional love is possible. Balancing the risks, might the disease appear in the planned donor child?

For poorer parents, who cannot afford genetic testing to eliminate poor matching embryos, it will surely be the case that some newborns will not be viable bone marrow donors. Marissa Ayala for example, had only a 25 percent chance of being a compatible donor. It is also possible that the mother's health will be compromised in the process. If a mother learns that a baby isn't the right match, is the child abortable? Legally, perhaps so depending on the trimester in which this is discovered, but morally, even for privacy and abortion proponents, aborting viable healthy fetuses simply because they are not the "right match" may expand the abortion battleground into murkier territory. Such medical procedures may also be criminal, given recent state legislative enactments, which criminalize harm to viable fetuses, whether due to a mother's drug use or her unwillingness to undergo a cesarean birth operation to prevent the death of a fetus. The potential risks and legal ramifications remain incalculable.

Recipients and Donors
Are Affected Psychologically

Reproductive altruism creates natural hierarchies; one child is born a supplier or healer and the other special or sacred. Turned on its head, the supplier becomes a household miracle worker or savior, but both siblings are victims of unfortunate circumstances. [As cited by Cora Cheyette] in a recent study, researchers found that organ recipients who had received a donation from a living donor were less comfortable about the charitable act, feeling burdened by the "debt."

> The children were depressed, complained of recurrent nightmares, had overdeveloped fears of hospitals and needles and had a constant sense of dread that the experience might be repeated. This was true for both siblings who donated and siblings who did not donate. The siblings who donated, however, were more withdrawn, anxious, depressed and had a lower sense of self-esteem, which the researchers attributed to a guilty fear that their tissue might not be "good enough." Other researchers have similarly warned that if the child turns out to be an incompatible donor or the transplant is unsuccessful, '[t]he . . . guilt which may follow in the wake of [that] failure could be transferred to the donor child with untoward effects, either in early bonding or later, as the child grows up under the shadow of having failed in an important task.

Donors were particularly uneasy about transplants from children. Other studies reveal a connection between the donee's health and the psychological well-being of the donor. UCLA [University of California Los Angeles] researchers discovered that donors were negatively affected by the recipients' postoperative quality of health. What the study could not reveal is whether donors would have suffered similar psychological distress had they not donated. Also, it would be useful to know from where the stress derives. For example, was donor stress linked to feelings of sympathy or guilt about the quality of the tissue donation?

What neither of the aforementioned studies nor any other has determined are the long-term psychological effects on child sibling donors. One that comes close, however, is a study conducted by researchers at the University of California at San Francisco who explored the psychological significance of donation among children who supplied bone marrow for another sibling. Most siblings, whether donors or not, according to their finding, experienced some form of stress and depression. Some of the donors experienced nightmares connected with the bone marrow harvesting process, becoming fearful of hospitals and needles. According to researchers, 33 percent of the donors suffered posttraumatic stress disorder-type symptoms at some point after donating. Sibling donors were also more likely to have a compromised sense of worth, suffer bouts of anxiety, and be withdrawn.

Thus, the notion that children donors are psychologically benefited from donating organs deserves serious scrutiny. Psychological benefit for the child donor is not an absolute. The possibility that the children donors experience relief for their recovering sibling seems likely; that would also appear to be true for nonsibling donors and other family members. Parents are probably more likely to be psychologically benefited by their children receiving an organ or tissue donation, which in part explains parental motivation for reproductive altruism. The UCLA and UC-San Francisco studies offer a different view of posttransplant psychology and relationships. Their analyses highlight fault lines in jurisprudence on compelled donations, indicating that courts have misinterpreted immediate psychological relief, satisfaction, and possibly joy with long-term sibling relationships. The studies seem to refute the underlying message that strong, healthy, psychological rela-

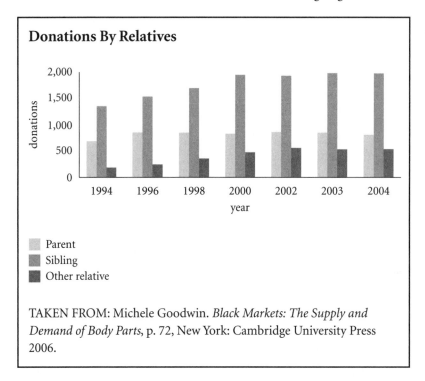

Donations By Relatives

TAKEN FROM: Michele Goodwin. *Black Markets: The Supply and Demand of Body Parts*, p. 72, New York: Cambridge University Press 2006.

tionships develop between donors and recipient siblings. The mistaken assumption could be explained by urgent desires to assist innocent children suffering from organ failure. [Amy] Waterman at the Washington University School of Medicine suggests that more psychosocial interventions are necessary to address the tensions involved with living donations.

Understanding the Role of Medicine

I have provided a glimpse of the dynamics through reported law and media cases. These however, do not represent unpublished legal opinions, cases without reports, family conflicts that never appear before a judge, nor the genetic or natural births motivated by reproductive altruism, which are simply not adjudicated. With the precedent established by *Strunk* [*Strunk v. Strunk*] and its progeny, concerns about the legality of parental consent for minors to undergo nontherapeutic extractive surgeries for the benefit of their siblings is also reduced. Thus, we see a reduction in petitions requesting declaratory judgments seeking consent for bone marrow and kidney transplants.

After *Strunk* and its progeny, important questions remain unanswered as to the breadth of the ruling. These include the roles of doctors and medicine. Is the role of medicine to prolong life as long as possible? How do we manage potential conflicts of interests, including physician involvement in the decision-making processes, where they have pecuniary and research interests? Biotechnology transports us to types of medical research unforeseeable and uncharted 30 years ago. The human genome was yet to be mapped, and bioprospecting had relevance only for plants and wildlife, not human beings as we see now. Technology was less sophisticated and its robust economic potential was yet to be fully appreciated. From this perspective, *Curran* [*Curran v. Bosze*], *Strunk*, and *Hart* [*Hart v. Brown*] were possibly short-term solutions to problems on a much grander scale. We must also chart the rights of children and the disabled too, which have developed in more sophisticated ways over the past quarter century. With parental immunity challenged in some jurisdictions, the possibility to ward off subsequent privacy and tort lawsuits from children harmed psychologically or physically by nonconsensual organ, tissue, or cell removal may be less guaranteed.

Exclusive reliance on altruism to meet increasing demand for sophisticated, life-saving medical therapies forces strains on the system, and drives individuals to create unregulated, living-donor subsystems, some which are legal and others that are not. The altruism subsystems, including compelled living donations and reproductive altruism, operate on principles inapposite to the legal values associated with altruism. The subsystems lack voluntariness, informed consent, and mutual bargaining power, subverting the intention of altruism, with heightened possibilities for coercion, pressure, guilt, and unequal positioning. Thus, these systems are overshadowed by ethical, moral, and even legal doubts. As discussed earlier, this jurisprudence must become more nuanced in light of the potential for confusion, manipulation, and other cases to which this line of legal thought might be applied.

Currently, siblings account for more contributions to the living donor pool than any other groups. Most sibling donors are adults; however, minor siblings continue to be represented among living donors. OPTN [Organ Procurement and Transplantation Network] does not indicate the relationship to the donee of child donors under 10 years old. Yet, as described earlier, the margins by which siblings contribute are substantially greater than all other relatives. Siblings' contributions to the altruistic pool are double that of parents. Nonetheless, the dynamics behind the donations are difficult to monitor. . . .

Important Considerations for Sibling Donation

A social contract functions only when mutual bargaining power and beneficial reciprocity exist. The benefits need not be equal, but should be of some tangible value to both parties. It also seems important that individuals be allowed to express their generosity and humanity in ways that at times may infringe on their liberties, including bodily integrity and privacy in the aid of another. Therefore, it would be unwise to prophylactically proscribe individuals from participating in living donation, even some children. There must, however, be a balance beyond the tests previously established.

First, it must be clearly understood that compelled living donations from children and incompetent persons are the least desired forms of donation. Donations from persons legally incompetent cannot easily fit under the umbrella of altruism; the heightened probability for compromising their humanity and dignity makes it so. We must consider alternatives for desperate parents and siblings beyond the reach of the most vulnerable members of their families. Currently, federally mandated altruism procurement constrains their ability to seek alternative, viable sources domestically. Again, the weaker, less desirable options become the exclusive options, quite unnecessarily. Conversely, those suspicious of the American transplantation system lack the confidence and motivation to participate in the current altruistic regime as donors, but it is possible other systems might prove more attractive to them. Let us remember that children and the mentally ill are not viable replacements for an incompetent, ineffective, organ procurement system. Their participation should be limited to the narrowest possibilities.

Second, minors younger than 13 years old should be proscribed from participating in living donation procedures. An age barrier would be no different than those imposed in labor or employment systems. Children under 13 lack the capacity to substantially appreciate the nuances of these transactions, including potential future health risks. This may also be true for teenagers; however, it is more likely that teenagers will be more literate, knowledgeable, educable, and aware than 7-year-olds. Their understanding of the transplantation process will be more substantive than symbolic, resulting in meaningful dialogues about risks and benefits of tissue and organ harvesting. Age should not be the only criteria, less it become an arbitrary element. Courts should borrow from the Tort common law by examining the child's experience and intelligence.

Third, a guardian *ad litem* should always be appointed. Fourth, family and independent counseling must be required to ensure that parents understand the dynamics of the depth of their actions and long-term consequences. Fifth, an independent physician must be appointed for the prospective donor to avoid conflicts of interest. Finally, a statement should be issued to the court from the donor as to why she desires to participate as an organ or tissue donor. Limiting the participation of children will reduce the pool of viable organs, and other solutions must be sought.

Periodical Bibliography

The following articles have been selected to supplement the diverse views presented in this chapter.

John L. Allen Jr.	"The Nightmare Scenario of Organ Donation," *National Catholic Reporter*, November 16, 2007.
Paul Garwood	"Dilemma Over Live-Donor Transplantation," *Bulletin of the World Health Organization*, January 2007.
Harvard Reviews of Health News	"Organ Donation for People with HIV," 2006.
Lisa Hitchen	"No Evidence That Presumed Consent Increases Organ Donation," *British Medical Journal*, September 11, 2008.
Calixto Machado, et al.	"The Concept of Brain Death Did Not Evolve to Benefit Organ Transplants," *Ethics*, April 2007.
Trish Morrissey	"The Dilemma of Donation," *Emergency Nurse*, February 9, 2008.
Rachel Nowak and Linda Geddes	"Not Brain-Dead, but Ripe for Transplant," *New Scientist*, August 4, 2006.
John B. Shea	"Cardiac Arrest, Brain Death, and Organ Donation: The Inconvenient Truth," *Catholic Insight*, September 2007.
Rob Stein	"New Trend in Organ Donation Raises Questions," *The Washington Post*, March 18, 2007.
Robert D. Truog	"Organ Donation Without Brain Death?" *Hastings Center Report*, November-December 2005.
Graeme Wood	"Let's Harvest the Organs of Death Row Inmates," *GOOD Magazine*, February 2008.

OPPOSING
VIEWPOINTS®
SERIES

CHAPTER 4

What Is the Future
of Organ Donation?

Chapter Preface

For people in need of a new organ, their only viable option currently is to receive one from a human donor. However, scientific advances may make other donor sources possible in the future, such as the creation of artificial organs or the use of animals as donors. One possibility that may emerge is the elimination of donors entirely, by cloning the person's own organs. This type of cloning, which is considered therapeutic cloning (as opposed to reproductive cloning, which is almost universally opposed), is not yet possible, but some believe it could one day drastically improve the lives of people who desperately require a new organ.

The organ cloning process would first entail extracting DNA from the patient and inserting it into an enucleated egg. The embryonic stem cells that form after the egg begins to divide could then be used to generate an organ that is a perfect genetic match to the patient. At this time, however, efforts to clone human embryos have been largely unsuccessful. Some achievement has been made in creating and transplanting cloned heart and kidney tissues in cows, an indication that the science behind organ cloning is viable. Scientists have also been able to remove stem cells from cloned mice and monkey embryos. However, many people have their doubts that these efforts will yield positive results for humans. As ethicist Wesley J. Smith observes, "It takes about 100 tries to obtain one viable cloned mouse embryonic stem cell line. . . . Even if we decided to strictly ration therapeutic cloning to, say, the sickest 100,000 patients, you would still need 10 million eggs!"

The use of embryonic stem cells is also controversial because many people believe that the destruction of these embryos is akin to abortion. This view is not universally shared— Rudolph Jaenisch of the Whitehead Institute in Cambridge, Massachusetts, writing on behalf of the President's Council on

Bioethics, argues that the embryos used in therapeutic cloning have virtually no potential to become normal human beings. If cloned organs can one day be created using adult stem cells, such concerns could become less relevant.

The future of organ donation is limited only by human imagination and technology. The authors in this chapter evaluate alternatives to traditional organ donation.

"It is . . . an exciting time for xenotrans- plantation and its potential applica- tions in the treatment of clinical and neurological disorders."

Animal-to-Human Organ Transplants Can Be Successful

Roger Barker

In the following viewpoint, Roger Barker asserts that xenotrans- plantation, or the transplanting of animal organs and tissues into other animals (typically humans), is a promising medical advancement. Barker acknowledges that the risks of organ rejec- tion and infection have thus far limited the use of animal or- gans. However, Barker contends, the risk of diseases has been overstated and research to increase the survival of transplanted organs has had some success. Barker is a university lecturer in neurology at the Cambridge Centre for Brain Repair, located in the United Kingdom.

As you read, consider the following questions:

1. What is zoonotic infection, as defined by Barker?

2. According to the author, what will be necessary to over- come the rejection of animal organs?

Roger Barker, "The Future of Organ Transplant," www.bluesci.org, no. 4, Michaelmas 2005. Reproduced by permission.

3. According to Barker, what did data collected by Khazal
Paradis and his associates demonstrate?

The shortage of organs and tissues for donation has made
xenotransplantation [transplanting organs or tissue from
one species to another] a realistic approach for the treatment
of organ failure and disease. In the context of human xenotransplantation, it is envisaged that in the future, whole organs (heart, kidney) or tissue (pancreatic, islet cells or neural
tissue) from pigs may be transplanted into human recipients.
The comparable size of pig organs to their human equivalents
and ease of breeding makes this animal the optimal donor for
xenotransplants. These features also facilitate research into the
immunology of xenograft rejection, and have led to the development of a number of genetically engineered pig lines.

Addressing the Problem of Organ Rejection

Transplantation of tissue from one species to another carries
two major problems, which are the focus of that research of
numerous laboratories. The first is immunological rejection
and the second is the risk of zoonotic infection (diseases com-
municable from animals to humans). Rejection of transplanted
tissue has proven to be a major obstacle in all experimental
studies to date. Porcine tissue expresses a number of specific
epitopes (proteins and carbohydrates on the surface of cells)
which trigger a very brisk human immune response. In the
case of whole organ transplants, the rejection process mounted
by the host is hyperacute and takes place in a matter of seconds or minutes. The main mediators of this rejection process
are pre-formed human antibodies, which react with the
epitopes on the transplanted organ, leading to rapid and irreversible damage of the blood vessels, ischaemia (inadequate
oxygen delivery) and death of the transplanted organ. In order
to overcome this rejection process, powerful immunosuppressive drugs, similar to those used for allografting (human-to-
human transplants), would be necessary. Immunosuppressive

treatments for xenotransplants would need to be much more aggressive than those currently adopted prior to allografts, which already put patients in a susceptible position when fighting opportunistic infections.

Strategies aiming to modify the transplanted porcine tissue so it becomes less immunogenic are increasingly successful. They involve genetically engineering the porcine tissue, either to express factors that suppress the host immune response or to remove the epitopes that drive immune rejection. In the first case, this has been achieved by generating porcine tissue capable of expressing inhibitors of the human complement cascade, a series of proteins whose activation in adverse immune reactions leads to rapid loss of tissue. This work was pioneered by David White and colleagues at Imutran, a company originally based here in Cambridge. The second strategy, mainly undertaken by David Cooper and David Sachs at Massachusetts General Hospital in Boston, has involved removing the major immunogenic epitope in pig tissue, called alpha 1, 3-galactosyltransferase. Using this approach, the survival of transplanted organs has been extended in experimental studies but is by no means long lasting. To date, successful transplants using baboons have only prolonged the life of pig organs for months rather than years, but this does not exclude the very real possibility that modified animal organs may be one day used in the clinic.

Reducing the Risk of Infection

The second major issue concerning xenotransplantation is the spread of infection, which at its simplest level can be in the form of bacteria and viruses commonly found in farm-bred animals. This is a particular problem for transplant recipients, whose immune systems are already weakened by the stress of invasive surgery and the drugs used to prevent rejection of the donor organ. The risk of such infections can be dramatically reduced if the animals are raised in special quarantine condi-

Xenotransplantation Is Not Immoral

There is nothing inherently immoral with transplanting animal organs into humans, assuming all aspects of good medical care and bioethics have been followed.

The Pontifical Academy for Life, in *Prospects for Xenotransplantation* (2001), addressed this issue specifically:

> From our point of view, supported by the biblical perspective that asserts that every person is created "in the image and likeness of God" (Gen 1: 26–27), we reaffirm that humans have a unique and higher dignity. However, humans must also answer to the Creator for the manner in which they treat animals. As a consequence, the sacrifice of animals can be justified only if required to achieve an important benefit for society, as is the case with xenotransplantation of organs or tissues.

> *Richard Benson, "Human and Animal Hybrids? Genetic Enhancement?" April 11, 2008. www.the-tidings.com.*

tions. A more serious concern, however, relates to viruses that could spread from the pig and cause disease in humans. In particular, a class of viruses known as porcine endogenous retroviruses (PERVs) do not cause disease in pigs but could spread into the human recipient. Such infection could theoretically trigger a hitherto unknown disease in much the same way as has been postulated for the spread of AIDS from nonhuman primates, but based on tests on more than 160 patients who have been exposed to living porcine tissue, there is no evidence to support such risk. Data reported in 1999 by Khazal Paradis and colleagues at Imutran clearly demonstrated that, despite the presence of surviving pig cells years after transplantation, there was no evidence of infection or disease in human recipients. In contrast, subsequent studies, notably by Luc van der Laan and colleagues in California, have included transplantation of pig tissue into severe combined immunodeficient (SCID) mice to show that the PERVs can spread throughout the host's body. In these mice there are no overt signs of disease, but clearly the fact that PERVs can escape and spread under such circumstances is a cause for concern. Still, it should be noted that immunosuppression in organ recipients is much less powerful than that seen with SCID mice.

A further uncertainty is whether pig organs and tissues have the capacity to perform the functions of their human equivalent with comparable efficiency. Research suggests that this may depend on the specific organs. Xenotransplantation of liver, for example, could be problematic because of the large number of essential and often species-specific proteins produced, whereas there is no reason to believe that pig dopamine neurons could not be used in patients with Parkinson's disease, as the grafted cells should be able to produce the missing dopamine in sufficient concentrations to mediate a positive effect. Moreover, in terms of neurodegenerative disorders, rejection following transplantation of pig tissue into the brain has been shown to be much slower than with whole organs. This process relies less on antibodies and the complement cascade and more on the other effector of the immune system, namely the T cells. While these cells do contribute to the chronic rejection of organ transplants in xenotransplantation, it seems possible that the engineering of neural tissue coupled to a strong immunosuppressive therapy would enable neural tissue to be grafted successfully into the adult brain of patients with neurological disorders.

The recent development of transgenic pig lines has enabled the field of xenotransplantation to advance yet closer to the clinic. As our understanding of the complex immune reactions induced by xenografts improve, so do strategies to overcome rejection. In the field of neural transplantation, emerging data suggests that cells transplanted from one species into another may have a primary advantage over their allografted equivalent. For example, xenografted pig cells appear to have a greater capacity to grow processes and migrate within the adult rodent brain than rodent cells of the same type. If this proves to be the case, then xenografted tissue would have great potential to replace cells lost in neurological conditions, as well as to recreate circuits through long-distance neuronal connections. It is, therefore, an exciting time for xenotransplantation and its potential applications in the treatment of clinical and neurological disorders.

| "After decades of research, xenotransplantation has proved to be an extremely costly failure that may pose serious health risks to the public."

Animal-to-Human Organ Transplants Are a Failure

People for the Ethical Treatment of Animals UK

In the following viewpoint, People for the Ethical Treatment of Animals UK (PETA UK) contends that animal organs cannot be safely or successfully transplanted into humans. According to PETA UK, xenotransplantation experiments, where animal organs and tissues were transplanted into other species including humans, have failed for decades and have not extended lives beyond a few months. In addition, the organization argues, the animals in these experiments are treated cruelly, and implanting their organs into humans may lead to deadly epidemics. PETA UK is an animal rights organization that opposes the use of animals by humans for any reason, including food and experimentation.

People for the Ethical Treatment of Animals UK, "Xenotransplants: Killing Humans and Animals," peta.org.uk, 2003. Reproduced by permission.

As you read, consider the following questions:

1. According to the authors, what percentage of human-to-human organ transplants fail or are rejected within five years?
2. Which viruses have passed from primates to humans, as stated by the organization?
3. How long did Baby Fae live after her baboon heart transplant, as stated by the authors?

Xenotransplants are surgical procedures in which the "donor" and recipient are members of different species. During the past century, there have been many attempts to carry out animal-to-human transplants, but all have failed, with patients generally surviving only a few minutes, hours or days. Transplantation of vital organs and other body parts, such as bone marrow taken from non-human animals, has been attempted as part of experimental treatments for degenerative organ diseases and organ failure and for diseases such as AIDS and Parkinson's disease. After decades of research, xenotransplantation has proved to be an extremely costly failure that may pose serious health risks to the public.

A Horrible Experience for Animals

Animals raised for their organs are subjected to the sensory deprivation of a sterile laboratory and denied all social interaction with members of their own species. When it becomes time for them to "donate" their organs, they are killed.

Researchers described monkeys and baboons who were recipients of organs from another species dying after fits of vomiting and diarrhoea. These animals also suffered from violent spasms, bloody discharge, grinding teeth and uncontrollable, manic eye movements.

In one lab, "Baboon W201m", an organ recipient, died of a stroke after two days of limb spasms and paralysis. A genetically modified pig's heart was welded to vital arteries in the neck of "Baboon W205m". Researchers noted that his heart was swelling beyond its natural size and that strange yellow fluid was seeping from the transplanted organ. He was "sacrificed" after 21 days.

Failed Science

Xenotransplantation has a disastrous record, but rather than abandoning this line of experimentation, researchers have begun to genetically manipulate donor animals in an attempt to make the organs more acceptable to recipients. Pigs are currently being manipulated to carry human genes, even though scientists still do not know the functions of all human genes, and researchers can only speculate about the mapping of pigs' genes. The future of xenotransplantation appears to be just as disastrous as its past.

The human immune system is designed to identify and reject foreign objects. Human-to-human transplants have relied on immunosuppressive drugs to prevent rejection, yet 50 per cent of transplanted organs still fail or are rejected within five years. Genetic differences can cause an even more violent rejection that destroys the new organ within minutes. Scientists have developed increasingly powerful immunosuppressive therapies to overcome this natural reaction, but a suppressed immune system obviously leaves the recipient vulnerable to potentially fatal infections.

Decades of Failure

In 1963, surgeon Thomas Starzl grafted baboon kidneys into six patients. They survived from 19 to 98 days.

The advent of Cyclosporin, an immunosuppressant drug, gave researchers a greater chance of success. In 1977, a 25-year-old woman in South Africa was given a baboon heart. It worked for six hours.

In 1984, a newborn baby received a baboon heart in California. She lived for 20 days.

In the early 1990s, Dr. Thomas Starzl of the University of Pittsburgh transplanted baboon livers into two patients who had advanced hepatitis B, reasoning that since the hepatitis virus does not cause liver damage in baboons, a baboon liver would increase their chances of survival. One patient lived 70 days, the other, 26. Because of the large doses of immunosuppressive drugs needed to prevent rejection of the primate organ, both died from infection.

In 1995, AIDS patient Jeff Getty received transplanted bone marrow taken from a baboon. Baboons infected with the human immunodeficiency virus (HIV), presumed to cause AIDS, do not develop the life-threatening immune deficiency that characterises human AIDS. Bone marrow is an important component of the immune system, and Getty's doctors hypothesised that by transferring this component to their patient, they could create a "parallel" immune system that would fight the virus. Just two weeks after the transplant, doctors were forced to admit that the experiment had been a failure and that no trace of baboon cells could be found in the patient.

Throughout the 1990s, a biotech company called Imutran claimed that it was on the cusp of solving the crucial issue of organ rejection, which has prevented trials on humans. In 1995, it made the claim that it would be ready to start transplanting pig hearts into humans within a year, yet the company's documents clearly show that its xenotransplantation programme has come "nowhere near to fulfilling its promises."

Hidden Dangers of Xenotransplantation

Because of the danger of unleashing new diseases into the human population, many in the scientific community are calling for a moratorium on all xenotransplants. Some viruses carried by pigs can be screened, but as experts point out, you cannot screen for diseases that you do not know about. Some porcine viruses can infect human cells and mutate. Ian Wilmut, the

"Good news Mr. Poindexter! We found a kidney donor!" Cartoon by Dan Rosandich. www.CartoonStock.com.

scientist who cloned Dolly the sheep, abandoned experiments that would have led to cloning pigs, citing concerns that pigs could harbour viruses that could be passed on to people.

There have been incidences in which viruses crossed from primates to humans—including filoviruses, Ebola and Marburg—with deadly results. Despite this, baboons are still considered "useful" for xenotransplantation.

In addition to known pathogens, animals may also harbour unidentified viruses, bacteria and parasites that could prove deadly to people. Many human epidemics can be traced to microbes "jumping" from one species to another. Examples include the following:

- Sin Nombre, a fatal hantavirus that attacks the lungs, is carried by rodents and has twice broken out during the 1990s in the southwest United States.

163

- In Australia, two dangerous new viruses have affected humans—Lyssavirus, from two species of bat, and Morbilli, a relative of the measles virus that killed 14 horses and two people.

- The Nipah outbreak, which killed at least 100 people in Malaysia, involved the transmission of a highly lethal, unidentified virus from pigs to humans.

Xenotransplantation Is Costly and Uncertain

Questions have been raised about whether seriously ill patients are given all the facts when considering xenotransplantation. Patients may not be aware that xenotransplantation has never been successful. In 1984, doctors at Loma Linda University in California transplanted a baboon heart into an infant named Fae, who was born with serious heart defects. Baby Fae died 21 days later. No human heart was sought for transplantation, and Baby Fae was not recommended for surgical repair, even though both these alternatives would have given her a better chance of survival.

Xenotransplantation is a costly business. Because this research is funded by the biotechnology industry, not charities or universities, these experiments are unlikely to be abandoned. The industry has already expended ample time and money in this area, so no matter what the cost in terms of human and animal lives, the industry will continue to try to recoup some of its investment. Analysts predict that a $6 billion a year market awaits the first firm that can prevent the human body from rejecting such organs.

While this avenue is being unsuccessfully explored, scientifically valid lines of research are being rejected, and people with life-threatening illnesses are dying.

The history of xenotransplantation makes its future uncertain. Stem cell research appears to be a promising new starting point and is set to become "the hope for the future" in this area.

Advocates of cross-species transplants, however, point to the scarcity of human organ donors to justify continued efforts in this field. Every year, thousands of Britons are buried with organs suitable for donation, far exceeding the 6,000 people currently on transplant waiting lists. In 2002, 414 people died while waiting for a suitable organ.

The policies of other European countries assume that, unless otherwise specified, every person is an organ donor. The burden rests with individuals or their families if they do not wish to donate their organs. In Britain, debate concerning the adoption of the same policy regularly arises. It is accepted that, in the future, we will also adopt an "opt-out" policy. In the meantime, carry a donor card. Since the success rate of xenotransplantation is nil, waiting for an 11th-hour human donor still offers a greater chance of survival for the patient.

> *"The idea of being able to create replacement organs from scratch . . . has considerable allure."*

Replacement Organs Can Be Grown

The Economist

In the following viewpoint, The Economist *magazine asserts that a possible alternative to organ transplants is to create replacement organs using the patient's own cells and tissues. According to the publication, replacement organs would eliminate the possibility of organ rejection. Although the magazine acknowledges this process is still in its early stages, it points out that the technology has been used to create artificial bladders and knee cartilage.* The Economist *is a weekly newsmagazine focusing on international politics and business news and opinion.*

As you read, consider the following questions:

1. According to the author, how many people are on the organ waiting list in the United States?

2. What are progenitor cells, as defined by the author?

3. According to *The Economist*, how many people have been treated with Carticel?

Today there are around 90,000 patients in America registered and waiting for organ transplants. Macabre as it sounds, they are, in effect, waiting for a genetically suitable, organ-donating somebody within a few hundred miles to die, and provide a replacement for a terminally damaged heart, kidney, liver, pancreas or other organ. But even those patients lucky enough to receive a donor organ in time, and survive the transplant surgery, face more misery still. Some will reject the new organ, and will be put back on the waiting list; those who do not will spend the rest of their lives on drugs that are prone to cause side-effects and will suppress their immune systems, preventing rejection but leaving them susceptible to infections and other maladies.

Most patients, however, never get even that far. Although most Americans support organ donation, very few go through the complicated process of formally consenting to it. Of those that do, not all are able to donate, either because their organs are unsuitable or their families decide to overrule their wishes—which is allowed under American law.

Replacement Organs Are Being Researched

So the idea of being able to create replacement organs from scratch, using a patient's own tissues—and hence preventing rejection—has considerable failure. Researchers including Robert Langer, of the Massachusetts Institute of Technology, and Anthony Atala, of the Wake Forest University Institute of Regenerative Medicine in Winston-Salem, North Carolina, are trying to do just that. Dr. Atala, a pioneer in the field, is now working with Tengion, a biotech firm based in King of Prussia, Pennsylvania. It is one of several firms pursuing the idea of making organs to order, but seems to have made the most progress. Already, a handful of patients in America have been quietly fitted with new bladders made using Dr. Atala's technology.

Artificial Organs Could Be Beneficial

Despite limited success with totally implanted devices, artificial organ research continues with devices such as the implantable membrane oxygenator, a type of "artificial lung" that helps oxygenate the blood of people suffering from acute respiratory distress syndrome. For the most part, most observers agree that artificial organ development is potentially beneficial for many patients. As with most aspects of medical care in the twenty-first century, issues of fair allocation and cost continue to be problematic. Some feel that putting a large medical effort into developing such machines may be placing too great an emphasis on "rescuing" patients who are among the most severely ill, thus reducing the emphasis on the utility of achieving the best medical outcomes for the most number of people in a fair manner.

David Petechuk, Organ Transplantation. *Westport, CT: Greenwood Press, 2006.*

The approach is simple, but it has taken decades to refine. Healthy progenitor cells (the precursors to particular cell types) are extracted from the patient, isolated, and multiplied in culture. They are then placed into a scaffolding structure, made of collagen, which is sculpted to resemble the required organ. This in turn is then placed into a soup of nutrients in an incubator, resembling an aquarium, that simulates the conditions found inside the human body. "Four to six weeks later, you have a 'neo-bladder' that can then be placed into the patient," says Dr. Atala. The immune system senses nothing untoward, allowing the body to stimulate the remaining growth necessary for full functionality. The collagen scaffolding is gradually reabsorbed into the body.

The idea of building body parts on a scaffold made of collagen by using a patient's own cells is not new. Genzyme, a biotech firm based in Boston, makes a product called Carticel, for example, which allows cartilage to be cultured in the laboratory from a patient's own cells and then implanted into the patient's knee to repair cartilage defects. Since its introduction in 1997, it has been used to treat more than 10,000 patients.

A Fast-Moving Field

But Tengion, which plans to put its neo-bladder into clinical trials later this year [2006], has loftier ambitions. Furthermore, it has the funds to pursue them, having raised $40m[illion] in initial funding late [in 2005]. While there is a lot of research in the field—dating back to a series of animal studies, co-written by Dr. Atala, which appeared in the journal *Nature Biotechnology* in 1999—no other commercial venture has yet got as far as developing a neo-bladder, let alone other, more complex organs.

The field is now moving fast. "Ten years ago, they said organs couldn't be built. Now the challenge is unravelling solid organs like the liver, pancreas, heart, and lungs," writes Christopher Thomas Scott, a bioethicist at Stanford University, in his recent book, *Stem Cells Now*. While the prospects for organs to order seem promising, however, there is no guarantee that what works in animals will also work in humans. Patients, doctors and investors should not get their hopes up until trials of Tengion's neo-bladder demonstrate that the new technology really can hold water.

> *"The transplantation of HIV-positive organs to HIV-positive patients is not a panacea for the ongoing shortage of organs."*

HIV-Positive Organs Can Be Transplanted into HIV-Positive Patients

Gregory W. Rutecki

In the following viewpoint, Gregory W. Rutecki opines that one way to address the organ shortage is by transplanting HIV-positive organs into HIV- positive patients. According to Rutecki, this solution would have safeguards to ensure that HIV-positive organs are not transplanted into uninfected patients and that the operating team would not be at risk of infection. Although these transplantations would be limited in scope, Rutecki asserts that they would be a promising step in the future of organ donation. Rutecki is the director of medical education at Mount Carmel Health System in Columbus, Ohio.

As you read, consider the following questions:

1. What is the "gerrymandered" definition of death, as explained by Rutecki?

Gregory W. Rutecki, "Transplanting HIV-Positive Organs into HIV-Positive Patients," *Center for Bioethics and Human Dignity*, August 27, 2004. Reproduced by permission.

2. According to the author, what percentage of HIV-infected individuals also have Hepatitis C?

3. According to Rutecki, how does the program he discusses stratify HIV-positive organ recipients?

It would be refreshing to critique an organ donation plan that would increase supply without simultaneously violating ethical constraints. The law of supply and demand has imposed unforgiving rules on solid organ transplantation. As a result, there has been a flurry of activity aimed at the problem. Unfortunately, efforts to date have been disturbing in a number of ways.

Roadblocks to Donation

First, there were asystolic protocols, characterized by ethicist Renee Fox as "an ignoble form of cannibalism." In these protocols, the "dead donor rule" (i.e., organs may only be taken from patients who have died; patients may not be killed to allow for organ procurement) was challenged by a "gerrymandered" definition of death (two minutes without a heartbeat). That definition, not new to transplantation, was initially maligned (the University of Pittsburgh Protocol in the mid 1990s, for example), but has now, with minor changes, been accepted by many. The engendered confusion inhabited contingent efforts to retrieve organs from anencephalic infants. Donors who were dying and donors who were dead were thus treated the same. An increase in supply occurred, but at the expense of donor dignity.

In other ways—at least in its early stages—living, adult liver transplantation stumbled over ethical hurdles of its own. The technical "learning curve" was complicated by the determination of optimum graft size. Estimating volume so that donor and recipient had enough liver tissue to survive after surgery was, to say the least, tricky. As a result, in some centers, recipient need trumped the long honored "primum non

A New Group of Potential Organ Donors

[Organs] would need to be taken from people with HIV who are otherwise healthy—for example, people with early stages of HIV who died in motor vehicles accidents.... But it's important to remember that the need for such organs overwhelms the supply. On average sixteen Americans—with and without HIV—die each day awaiting an organ transplant. That's why any way to find a new group of potential organ donors makes sense.

"Organ Donation for People with HIV,"
Harvard Reviews of Health News, *2006.*

nocere," or first do no harm. Organ supply again increased, but donors were again harmed. Some *donors* ultimately required liver transplants, and others died as a direct result of donation.

Recently, market forces have been suggested as a critical supply-side component in the organ donation equation. They have begun to "re"-intrude themselves on an enterprise that has heretofore valued covenantal giving. Will there be an ethical downside to modest reimbursement for donation? In India, paid donors' quality of life has been poor and "middlemen" brokering transplant deals can make more than donors.

The need for more organs will not go away. Indeed, need is likely to intensify with each passing year. As the technique of medicine improves (more people living longer), and certain disease populations increase (Hepatitis C-induced liver disease, for example), the crisis will become more critical. As a result, the call for new programs to increase donors will continue.

Matching HIV-Positive Organs and Recipients

July 15, 2004, brought a unique proposal to the organ supply debate: transplanting HIV-positive organs into HIV-positive recipients. Since HIV patients are living longer in the current era of Highly Active Anti-Retroviral Therapy (HAART), and since their risk for organ failure from associated diseases and treatments is substantial, they can benefit from solid organ transplantation. Individuals infected with HIV who are co-infected with Hepatitis C are but one example. Prevalent statistics for this specific co-infection put the rate as high as 92 percent. The survival gains made in this population as a result of HAART are more than offset by two problems resulting from Hepatitis C. First, the progression of liver disease is accelerated, and second, patients do worse with standard therapy for Hepatitis C. The increased occurrence of cirrhosis and liver mortality that results can only be mitigated by transplantation.

What ethical issues, however, lurk beneath the surface of this proposal? The legislation passed in Illinois that would permit the policy change has been signed into law. The decision has been hailed as one way to expand the base of potential but scarce donors. The claim of lifesaving therapy without an ethical downside seems too good to be true. Specific questions must be answered. Are recipient risks, including graft-transmitted viral resistance and deterioration from immune suppression, factored into the proposal? Is "redundancy" so built into the process that it will minimize the risk of "big" mistakes, such as HIV-positive organs being given to patients who are not HIV-positive? Is there adequate safety oversight? Are further assaults made on the definition of death and donor dignity?

Potential viral resistance has been dealt with appropriately. The donors would be individuals who have not received HAART therapy, and therefore would not transmit resistant viral strains. Recipients are also carefully chosen based on T cell counts (100 mm3 for liver recipients, 200 for kidney) so that they can safely tolerate immune suppression. Informed consent is explicit both in regards to the source of the organs as well as the innovation's "infancy" so-to-speak, so that recipient dignity is protected. No overwhelming technical or medical hurdles have appeared.

What about the dire possibility that an HIV-positive organ may be transplanted into a patient who is not infected with HIV? Redundancy has been built into the process so that "sign-offs" (note the plural) in the blood bank make such an adverse event most unlikely. The program is even designed to stratify HIV-positive patients who are in need of a transplant by MELD [model for end-stage liver disease] score, a standard that frees allocation decisions from social valuation. Patients on the waiting list for solid organs will not be harmed, for they simply could not receive the HIV-positive organs.

Is the operating team unnecessarily exposed to the risk of viral transmission? The current generation of surgeons has matured in an era that frequently treats patients with transmissible diseases (both HIV and Hepatitis C), and therefore has been "schooled" in universal precautions. The number of transplants that will result from this innovation will probably be small, and the risks, which have been *de rigeur* for an entire generation of healthcare personnel, are not prohibitive.

The transplantation of HIV-positive organs to HIV-positive patients is not a panacea for the ongoing shortage of organs. The sponsors of the program have made no such claim. Rather, it will be small in scale. It should benefit individuals with HIV/AIDS who need organs and have otherwise reasonable viability. I suspect that asystolic criteria for the definition of death will still be applied, a persistent and serious issue, but in every other way, the model takes the requisite ethical concerns seriously. In so doing, it represents a refreshing change in a troublesome ethical arena.

> *"Much of the transplant tourism and Internet solicitation processes occur beyond the laws and structures governing organ transplantation in the United States."*

The Internet and Transplant Tourism Are Questionable Sources for Organs

Liliana M. Kalogjera

In the following viewpoint, Liliana M. Kalogjera asserts that the future of organ transplant will entail finding sources for organs beyond the traditional waiting lists. According to Kalogjera, two emerging ways to procure organs are by traveling to countries where organ transplants are less costly and by using the Internet to find organ matches. However, Kalogjera notes, both of these alternatives raise important ethical concerns. Kalogjera is a staff attorney at the U.S. Department of Veterans Affairs Office of Regional Counsel in Milwaukee, Wisconsin.

As you read, consider the following questions:

1. How much do kidney transplant tours cost, according to the author?

2. According to an American Medical Association report cited by the author, what are some of the health risks associated with traveling after surgery?

3. According to Kalogjera, what do proponents of Internet solicitation claim is its utilitarian benefit?

The organ shortage continues to grow despite multifaceted efforts to increase the transplant organ supply. Some of these strategies, such as emotionally charged advertisements sponsored by organ procurement agencies, appeal to the general public's altruism. Others are market-based, such as proposals to overhaul existing U.S. laws to permit the sale of solid organs. Others focus on pragmatic directives, such as improving education about organ donation and streamlining the procedural aspects of organ donor registration (e.g., informational pamphlets and organ donor stickers on drivers' licenses).

Because these more traditional approaches have proved insufficient to address the growing crisis, novel alternatives continue to emerge and to create new ethical and legal dilemmas. Transplant tourism and Internet solicitation represent ways in which people are working around the legal restraints and institutional structures for obtaining an organ transplant in order to secure transplant organs themselves.

Transplant Tourism Is an Emerging Option

Transplant tourism involves travel to foreign countries for the purpose of obtaining an organ transplant. Transplant tourists hail from a variety of countries, including the United States, Germany, Israel, Japan, Australia, and Egypt. Destinations for transplant tourism include Colombia, China, the Philippines, India, and Thailand.

Organ transplant offerings vary among transplant tours. Organs may come from living or deceased donors and may include kidneys, hearts, lungs, and livers. Some transplant tourism companies, such as the Canadian-based MediTours, fall within the broader category of medical tourism and offer organ transplants as one option in a menu of other medical services, such as hip and knee replacements, orthodontics, plastic surgery, and in vitro fertilization. Others, such as Organ Transplant Services, which advertises an Arizona address, focus exclusively on organ transplants. In addition to providing the medical care associated with the organ transplant, transplant tours may include airfare, ground transportation, luxury accommodations, food, and other travel arrangements.

Advertised advantages of transplant tourism include access to organ transplants at a lower cost and with shorter waiting times than in countries such as the United States. Kidney transplant tours range from approximately $75,000 to $80,000, while liver tours may cost $100,000 or more. Some companies require an additional deposit in case of complications. The waiting time for a transplant organ for a transplant tourist may be shorter than in the United States because the transplant tourism destination has less restrictive or unenforced laws pertaining to the organ transplant process or because transplant tourists bypass the legal system entirely.

Transplant Tourism Can Save Money

Arguments supporting transplant tourism. Advocates for transplant tourism highlight the dire shortage of transplant organs in the United States and the cost savings associated with obtaining an organ transplant abroad. A person may be unable to obtain a life-saving transplant organ in time due to his or her position on the waiting list or due to an inability to pay for his or her share of health care costs related to the transplant. By expanding the organ supply, transplant tourism may help to relieve the shortage in the United States.

In light of these potential cost savings, at least one state legislature, West Virginia's, has introduced legislation to provide financial incentives for state employees to obtain medical care or procedures abroad when the following criteria are met:

(1) the care or procedures are less expensive in a foreign health facility, and (2) the total cost of the care or procedure plus the financial incentives does not exceed the cost of obtaining the care or procedure in the United States. Although the West Virginia legislation did not become law and was not specifically drafted to address transplant tourism, it may indicate some level of public support for facilitating transplant tourism by making it financially attractive and legitimating the practice.

Proponents also argue that transplant tourism provides a valuable public service. First, it brings together people who need organs and people who are willing to donate organs who would otherwise never meet in light of geopolitical boundaries that artificially divide the global supply of organs. Second, transplant tourism may have positive financial implications for individuals and for their families, communities, and even nations, many of whom are economically poor.

The Ethical Drawback
of Transplant Tourism

Despite the potential advantages of transplant tourism, critics emphasize its substantial drawbacks and risks.

Transplant tourism may pose health and safety risks to individual recipients and donors as well as from a public health perspective. To refute this claim, some transplant tourism companies advertise that their affiliated transplant hospitals are accredited by the Joint Commission International (a division of a subsidiary of the Joint Commission, which many regard as the premier accreditation body of hospitals in the United States) or that the transplant physicians have been trained in the United States. Although this may be true in some cases, because of the lack of oversight of transplant tourism, it is difficult, if not impossible, to ensure comparable health and safety standards to those within the United States. In addition, as pointed out in the American Medical

Association's June 2007 report entitled *Medical Travel Outside the United States*, travel after surgery may increase certain health risks, such as blood clots, and medical tourism raises infectious disease concerns. Furthermore, insufficient or illegible medical records may complicate the provision of follow-up care when transplant tourists return to their home countries.

From an ethical perspective, transplant tourism raises concerns about the potential exploitation of organ donors, which UNOS [United Network for Organ Sharing] and the World Health Organization [WHO] have highlighted in numerous statements denouncing transplant tourism. For example, the government of China, a transplant tourism destination, has admitted that executed prisoners have served as the primary organ source for its transplant program. The use of prisoners as donors contradicts ethical mandates that organ donation occur voluntarily, based on the autonomous choice of the donor or next of kin. Some news sources allege that these donors have not always been dead when the organ harvesting process began. Such a practice goes far beyond the realm of individual autonomy concerns and into the realms of torture and human rights abuses. Although the Chinese government claims to be developing a legal framework with safeguards, such as prohibitions on the sale of organs and organ trafficking, the results of these efforts remain to be seen.

Also ethically problematic are concerns about exploitation and coercion of donors through financial payments for organs. The living donors and families of deceased donors who supply organs for transplant tourism are often impoverished, and their recruitment process often lacks the disclosure and understanding of a truly informed consent process and the psychological screening process for living donors. A medical anthropological study concluded that, in addition to facing health problems due to insufficient follow-up care, many donors encounter psychological harm and social stigma due to their participation in the organ donation process. An individual interviewed in this study stated, "They call us prostitutes. . . . Actually, we are worse than prostitutes because we have sold something we can never get back. We are a disgrace to ourselves and to our country." Whether the donors are prisoners or impoverished people, it is ethically troublesome for people from the United States and other countries to bypass the ethical safeguards in their own countries in order to take advantage of lax laws and practices abroad.

Not only does transplant tourism potentially condone and promote the exploitation of vulnerable populations, it raises fairness and justice issues. A transplant tourist from the United States bypasses the waiting list and receives an organ based not on need, likelihood of success, or other medical factors, but because of ability to pay for and attend the transplant tour. This is problematic both in terms of fairness to others on the waiting list and, on a global level, in terms of justice in the allocation of organs.

Perhaps due to these ethical concerns, transplant tourism may face increased legal scrutiny in the future. Currently, many of the transplant tourism destinations lack adequate laws and enforcement mechanisms to regulate the practice. As such, anecdotal evidence suggests that, in many cases, transplant tourism bypasses the law entirely. This may prompt the countries of origin of transplant tourists to impose restrictions. Belgium, for example, has proposed to limit organ transplants from non-European Union hospitals to a list of hospitals deemed to meet certain ethical standards, such as informed consent requirements. Violators would be subject to a fine.

Finding Organs Online

Whereas transplant tourists travel the globe to obtain lifesaving organs, others find their match in a virtual community, such as MatchingDonors.com. Internet solicitation involves a

Leading Sources for Overseas Organs

India was a commonly known organ-exporting country, where organs from local donors are regularly transplanted to foreigners through sale and purchase. Although the number of foreign recipients seems to have decreased after the enactment of a law banning the organ trade (the Human Transplantation Act of 1994) the underground organ market is still existent and resurging in India. The Voluntary Health Association of India estimates that about 2,000 Indians sell a kidney every year. The drop in foreign recipients in India was accompanied by an increase in the number of foreign recipients in other countries, such as Pakistan and the Philippines.

In Pakistan, according to the Sindhi Institute of Urology, approximately 2,000 renal transplants were performed in 2005, of which up to two-thirds were estimated to have been performed on foreigners. In the Philippines, data obtained from the Renal Disease Control Program of the Department of Health, National Kidney Transplant Institute, show that of the 468 kidney transplants in 2003, 110 were for patients from abroad. There is no comparable data for Egypt but a considerable number of patients from neighbouring countries are believed to undergo organ transplantation there.

Yosuke Shimazano,
"The State of the International Organ Trade:
A Provisional Picture Based on Integration
of Available Information,"
Bulletin of the World Health Organization,
December 2007.

potential recipient and potential living donor finding each other on a Web site. At MatchingDonors.com, potential recipients pay a membership fee to post their photos and personal stories describing their transplant organ needs. Potential donors pay no fee and are able to browse the profiles of over 4,000 potential recipients. If a potential donor is interested in a potential recipient, the potential donor can contact the potential recipient to begin a dialogue and, if both agree, to proceed with the organ donation process. State and federal law in the United States permit directed living donation, although it has predominantly occurred between people who have a preexisting special relationship—such as family members or friends—not between people who met solely for the purpose of an organ exchange.

Proponents portray Internet solicitation as a "win-win" approach that provides a valuable public service by helping to match people in dire need for organs with altruistic potential donors in a manner that is safe, ethical, and legal. Matching-Donors.com displays numerous success stories in which a potential recipient and potential donor who met at the site exchanged a life-saving organ, and proponents point to MatchingDonors.com's tax-exempt status under Section 501(c)(3) of the Internal Revenue Code as general evidence of its ethically desirable nonprofit mission.

In terms of safeguards, to the extent organ transplants facilitated by Internet solicitation sites are performed in the United States, the transplant process benefits from the numerous medical and ethical protections implemented at hospitals nationwide. Because of the high quality of care at hospitals in the United States, donors and recipients—whether they meet through Internet solicitation or other means—are less vulnerable to the health and safety risks found in transplant tourism. In addition, many hospitals require psychological screening of live organ donors. This requirement provides an additional level of protection for donors and recipients and helps to balance out concerns about the lack of regulation of the Internet. Due to ethical or legal concerns, however, some hospitals have refused to perform transplants in which the donor and recipient met through Internet solicitation; this raises potential patient abandonment issues.

From an ethical perspective, Internet solicitation can help to promote individual autonomy and may be desirable on utilitarian grounds. Internet solicitation respects potential donors' rights to use their bodies as they see fit, to participate in charitable giving, and to receive emotional or psychological benefits from this gift. Internet solicitation also promotes the individual autonomy of potential recipients by providing them with a legal alternative to the waiting list. In particular, Internet solicitation gives potential recipients who lack willing or medically compatible family members or friends the opportunity to find a living donor. In addition, proponents set forth the utilitarian claim that Internet solicitation helps to increase the total number of organs, which helps the patients on the waiting list to advance faster up the list than they would in the absence of this alternative.

From a legal perspective, Internet solicitation is not, on its face, illegal at the state or federal level. Section 6(A) (3) of the 1987 version of the Uniform Anatomical Gift Act explicitly permits directed organ donation for transplantation purposes, and this permission is not contingent on how the donor and recipient met. Moreover, the communications underlying Internet solicitation may represent constitutionally protected speech under the First Amendment. To address potential legal concerns about the sale of organs, MatchingDonors.com boldly displays the prohibition on receipt of financial benefit in exchange for organ donation and recommends that any interested potential donor see his or her physician before matching.

Potential Problems of Internet Solicitation

UNOS and commentators from the bioethics and medical communities have expressed opposition to Internet solicitation for a variety of reasons.

First, despite acknowledgment of the legal prohibition on the exchange of valuable consideration for organ donation, critics have expressed concerns that recipients are, in fact, providing donors with financial or other consideration "under the table." Thus, Internet solicitation sites may be helping to facilitate circumvention of state and federal law as well as ethical prohibitions on organ sales.

Second, by bypassing the formal waiting list and allocation structure, Internet solicitation contributes to inequity in organ allocation. This argument is somewhat weakened by the fact that there is no formal waiting list or allocation structure for *living* organ donation in the United States. The practice of one family member donating an organ to another is a commonly accepted practice, and those recipients also bypass the waiting list for organs from deceased donors. Similarly, other types of directed living organ donation, such as between friends or fellow church members, also appear to have raised little ethical controversy in comparison to MatchingDonors. com. This leads to the question of whether the act of potential donors and recipients meeting on the Internet is ethically problematic in itself.

Critics do highlight various characteristics of the Internet forum of sites such as MatchingDonors.com as ethically problematic. First, on the Internet there may be an increased risk of recipient selection based on superficial or undesirable criteria, in a manner akin to a popularity or beauty contest or on the basis of racial or other prejudices. While this may be true, these concerns would apply to any directed donation arrangements in which the persons are not related; people are free to pick their friends on any basis they wish, superficial or not, and organ donation among friends does not appear to be as ethically controversial. Second, heightened concerns exist about the veracity of potential recipients' profiles. Because of the lack of legal and other safeguards of these Internet communities and the desperation of potential recipients, donors may participate under false pretenses. While this sort of deception is commonly accepted in other contexts—such as in the marketplace under the doctrine of *caveat emptor* (i.e., let the buyer beware)—the prohibition on organ sales suggests that the market perspective may be inappropriate for organs. This argument is particularly compelling because of the health and other risks that potential recipients face.

Two Novel Approaches

Certainly, transplant tourism and Internet solicitation represent two novel responses to the growing transplant organ shortage. Interestingly, the Internet, which has expanded individual access to information and communication in myriad ways, plays a key role for both strategies; transplant tourism companies rely on their Web presence to reach potential customers across the world, and Internet solicitation facilitates the introduction of potential donors and recipients who would otherwise never meet. Just as the Internet is largely unregulated, much of the transplant tourism and Internet solicitation processes occur beyond the laws and structures governing organ transplantation in the United States. As such, participants may be particularly vulnerable, which raises significant ethical concerns and may lead to the need for greater involvement of law and policy makers.

Periodical Bibliography

The following articles have been selected to supplement the diverse views presented in this chapter.

Tim Batchelder
"Organs, Commodities, Technologies," *Townsend Letter for Doctors & Patients*, October 2005.

Nell Boyce
"Down on the Organ Farm," *U.S. News & World Report*, June 16, 2003.

Jody A. Charnow
"Transplant Tourist Beware: Going to Another Country for a Kidney May Shorten Wait, But Hike Risks," *Renal & Urology News*, July 2006.

M.D. Dooldeniya and A.N. Warrens
"Xenotransplantation: Where Are We Today?" *Journal of the Royal Society of Medicine*, March 2003.

Joyce Frieden
"Online Organ Donor Matching Gaining Popularity," *Family Practice News*, November 15, 2005.

Toshi Knell
"A Perfect Storm of Dots," *Arena Magazine*, April-May 2006.

Vasudevan Mani
"Xenotransplantation: Animal Rights and Human Wrongs," *Ethics & Medicine*, Spring 2003.

Alexandra Moreno-Borchart
"Building Organs Piece by Piece," *EMBO Reports*, November 2004.

Nancy Scheper-Hughes
"Organs Without Borders," *Foreign Policy*, January-February 2005.

Yosuke Shimazono
"The State of the International Organ Trade," *Bulletin of the World Health Organization*, December 2007.

Elizabeth Svoboda
"2021: You'll Grow a New Heart," *Popular Science*, June 2006.

For Further Discussion

Chapter 1

1. After reading the viewpoints in this chapter, what do you think is the biggest obstacle to equitably allocating organs? Explain your answer, drawing from the viewpoints and any other relevant readings.

2. The U.S. Department of Health and Human Services addresses numerous myths about organ donation. Which, if any, of those misunderstandings do you think has had the greatest impact on potential organ donors? Why?

3. After reading Elizabeth Lynch's viewpoint, what steps do you think would be most effective in encouraging minorities and members of various faiths to increase organ donation? Do you agree with Lynch that religious leaders should play a key role? Explain your answers.

Chapter 2

1. After reading the viewpoints in this chapter, what approach do you think would be the best way to increase organ donation? Explain your answer.

2. Gary Becker is a Nobel Prize-winning professor of economics, while Sheila M. Rothman is a professor of public health and David J. Rothman directs the Center for the Study of Society and Medicine at the Columbia College of Physicians and Surgeons. Based on their credentials, which author(s) do you think is(are) best qualified to determine whether organs should be sold on the open market? Explain your answer.

Chapter 3

1. In his viewpoint, Gerald D. Coleman addresses several ethical issues surrounding organ donation. Of those issues, which, if any, are of greatest concern to you? Why?

2. J.L. Bernat and Leslie Whetstine, and their coauthors, disagree as to whether organ donation after cardiac death is ethical. Whose argument do you find more convincing? Why? Furthermore, do the authors' careers—neurology professor and philosophy professor, respectively—affect your response? Please explain.

3. L.D. de Castro's viewpoint on allowing prisoners to donate organs focuses on a policy in the Philippines. Do you think such an approach would work in the United States? Why or why not?

Chapter 4

1. Roger Barker and People for the Ethical Treatment of Animals UK disagree over the potential seriousness of viruses transmitted from animals to humans through xenotransplantation. Whose argument do you find more convincing and why?

2. After reading the viewpoint by *The Economist*, do you foresee a future in which organ donations are no longer necessary? Why or why not?

3. After reading the viewpoint by Liliana M. Kalogjera, would you travel to another country if you needed an organ? Do you think such travel is fair to the donor and the recipient? Explain your answer, drawing from the viewpoint and any other relevant readings.

Organizations to Contact

The editors have compiled the following list of organizations concerned with the issues debated in this book. The descriptions are derived from materials provided by the organizations. All have publications or information available for interested readers. The list was compiled on the date of publication of the present volume; the information provided here may change. Be aware that many organizations take several weeks or longer to respond to inquiries, so allow as much time as possible.

American Society of Law, Medicine & Ethics (ASLME)
765 Commonwealth Avenue, Suite 1634, Boston, MA   02215
(617) 262-4990 • Fax: (617) 437-7596
E-mail: info@aslme.org
Web site: www.aslme.org

The American Society of Law, Medicine & Ethics (ASLME) aims to provide high-quality scholarship and debate to professionals in the fields of law, health care, policy, and ethics. Among the issues the society addresses is organ donation. The society acts as a source of guidance and information through two quarterly publications, the *Journal of Law, Medicine & Ethics* and the *American Journal of Law & Medicine.*

American Society of Transplant Surgeons (ASTS)
2461 South Clark Street, Suite 640, Arlington, VA   22202
(703) 414-7870 • Fax: (703) 414-7874
Web site: www.asts.org

The purpose of the American Society of Transplant Surgeons (ASTS) is to promote education and research on organ and tissue transplantation through collaboration with public and private organizations. The society also seeks to enhance the quality of life of patients with end-stage organ failure. Videos on organ donation are available for purchase on the ASTS Web site.

Canadian Bioethics Society
561 Rocky Ridge Bay NW, Calgary, Alberta   T3G 4E7
  Canada
(403) 208-8027
E-mail: lmriddell@shaw.ca
Web site: www.bioethics.ca

The Canadian Bioethics Society is a nonprofit organization comprised of physicians, theologians, health care administrators, and other professionals with an interest in medical ethics, including the issues surrounding organ donation. The society promotes teaching and researching bioethics. It publishes a twice-yearly newsletter.

Center for Bioethics and Human Dignity
2065 Half Day Road, Deerfield, IL   60015
(847) 317-8180 • Fax: (847) 317-8101
E-mail: info@cbhd.org
Web site: www.cbhd.org

The Center for Bioethics and Human Dignity examines a variety of bioethical issues, including organ donation. Its explorations also consider the contribution of biblical values to modern Western culture. Articles are available on its Web site, including "Donor After Cardiac Death: What Is the Christian's Response?" and "The Internet and Stranger-to-Stranger Organ Donation: My Opinion."

The Hastings Center
21 Malcolm Gordon Road, Garrison, NY   10524-4125
(845) 424-4040 • Fax: (845) 424-4545
E-mail: mail@thehastingscenter.org
Web site: www.thehastingscenter.org

The Hastings Center is an independent research institute that explores the medical, ethical, and social ramifications of biomedical advances, including organ donation. The center publishes books, papers, guidelines, and the bi-monthly *Hastings Center Report*.

LifeSharers

6509 Cornwall Drive, Nashville, TN 37205

(888) 674-2688

Web site: www.lifesharers.com

LifeSharers is a nonprofit national network of organ donors. LifeSharers members promise to donate upon their death, and they give fellow members first access to their organs. Consequently, LifeSharers members have access to a greater number of organs. The organization publishes a monthly online newsletter.

National Minority Organ Tissue Transplant
Education Program

2041 Georgia Avenue NW, Washington, DC 20060

(202) 865-4888 • Fax: (202) 865-4880

Web site: www.nationalmottep.org

The aim of the National Minority Organ Tissue Transplant Education Program is to educate minority communities about transplantation and to increase minority participation in organ donation programs. It also seeks to reduce the number of minorities who require transplants by teaching preventive health care strategies. Statistics on organ donation and minority health issues and links to other organ transplantation Web sites are provided on its site.

Organ Procurement and Transplantation Network (OPTN)

PO Box 2484, Richmond, VA 23218

(804) 782-4730

Web site: www.optn.org

The Organ Procurement and Transplantation Network (OPTN) was established by the National Organ Transplant Act of 1984. The goal of the OPTN is to increase the supply of available organs and to make organ allocation more efficient and effective. Articles and news releases are available on its Web site.

President's Council on Bioethics

1425 New York Avenue NW, Suite C100
Washington, DC   20005
Phone: (202) 296-4669
E-mail: info@bioethics.gov
Web site: www.bioethics.gov

Founded in 2001, the President's Council on Bioethics advises the administration on bioethical issues, explores the ethical impact of biomedical and scientific research, and offers a forum for the discussion of these issues. Publications by the council include *Caring for Living Donors and Transplant Recipients: Five Policy Proposals* and *Organ Transplantation: Ethical Dilemmas and Policy Choices.*

Presumed Consent Foundation

PO Box 58, Plainview, TX   79073
Web site: www.presumedconsent.org

The mission of the Presumed Consent Foundation is to replace the current organ donation policy of the United States, which requires participants to "opt-in," with one that assumes that every person consents to being a donor unless they specifically opt-out. The foundation seeks to achieve this goal by educating the public about presumed consent policy and by advocating with politicians and government officials. Statistics about organ donation are available on its Web site.

Scientific Registry of Transplant Recipients (SRTR)

315 W. Huron Street, Suite 360, Ann Arbor, MI   48103
(800) 830-9664 • Fax: (734) 665-2103
Web site: www.ustransplant.org

The Scientific Registry of Transplant Recipients (SRTR) is administered by the Arbor Research Collaborative for Health with the University of Michigan. The registry analyzes data on organ transplantation and disseminates their findings to the transplant community. It issues an annual report, and statistics are also available on its Web site.

Uncaged Campaigns
5th Floor, Alliance House, 9 Leopold Street
Sheffield S1 2GY
United Kingdom
+44 (0) 114 272 2220
E-mail: info@uncaged.co.uk
Web site: www.uncaged.co.uk

Uncaged Campaigns works to end cruelty to animals, including the use of animals as organ donors. Ways it accomplishes this goal are e-mail campaigns and demonstrations. Links to articles about xenotransplantation are posted on the organization's Web site.

United Network for Organ Sharing (UNOS)
PO Box 2484, Richmond, VA   23218
(804) 782-4800 • Fax: (804) 782-4817
Web site: www.unos.org

The United Network for Organ Sharing (UNOS) was formed to help organ donors and people in need of organs locate each other. It also develops national policies on organ allocation. The organization publishes the monthly *UNOS Update*.

Bibliography of Books

David Price   *Organ and Tissue Transplantation.*
Aldershot, ed.   Burlington, VT: Ashgate, 2006.

Carol Ballard   *Organ Transplants.* Milwaukee, WI:
                   World Almanac Library, 2007.

Mark J. Cherry   *Kidney for Sale by Owner: Human
                   Organs, Transplantation, and the
                   Market.* Washington, DC:
                   Georgetown University Press, 2005.

Cecile Fabre   *Whose Body Is It Anyway? Justice and
                   the Integrity of the Person.* New York:
                   Oxford University Press, 2006.

John Farndon   *From Laughing Gas to Face
                   Transplants: Discovering Transplant
                   Surgery.* Chicago, IL: Heinemann
                   Library, 2006.

Judith Fox, ed.   *Kidney Transplantation: New
                   Research.* New York: Nova Science,
                   2006.

Michele Goodwin   *Black Markets: The Supply and
                   Demand of Body Parts.* New York:
                   Cambridge University Press, 2006.

Larry L. Hench   *Biomaterials, Artificial Organs and
and Julian R.   Tissue Engineering.* Boca Raton, FL:
Jones, eds.   CRC Press, 2005.

Susan E. Lederer   *Flesh and Blood: Organ
                   Transplantation and Blood Transfusion
                   in Twentieth-Century America.* New
                   York: Oxford University Press, 2008.

G. Wayne Miller — *The Xeno Chronicles: Two Years on the Frontier of Medicine Inside Harvard's Transplant Research Lab.* New York: PublicAffairs, 2005.

Ronald Munson — *Raising the Dead: Organ Transplants, Ethics, and Society.* New York: Oxford University Press, 2004.

David Petechuk — *Organ Transplantation.* Westport, CT: Greenwood Press, 2006.

Adam Schulman and Thomas W. Merrill, eds. — *Human Dignity and Bioethics: Essays Commissioned by the President's Council on Bioethics.* Washington, DC: President's Council on Bioethics, 2008.

Tina P. Schwartz — *Organ Transplants: A Survival Guide for the Entire Family: The Ultimate Teen Guide.* Lanham, MD: Scarecrow Press, 2005.

Lesley Alexandra Sharp — *Strange Harvest: Organ Transplants, Denatured Bodies, and the Transformed Self.* Berkeley, CA: University of California Press, 2006.

Henkie P. Tan, Amadeo Marcos, and Ron Shapiro, eds. — *Living Donor Transplantation.* New York: Informa Healthcare, 2007.

James Stacey Taylor — *Stakes and Kidneys: Why Markets in Human Body Parts Are Morally Imperative.* Burlington, VT: Ashgate Publishing, 2005.

Nicholas L. Tilney *Transplant: From Myth to Reality.* New Haven, CT: Yale University Press, 2003.

Stuart J. Youngner and Martha W. Anderson *Transplanting Human Tissue: Ethics, Policy, and Practice.* New York: Oxford University Press, 2004.

Index